CREATING & USING LEARNING TARGETS & PERFORMANCE SCALES

HOW TEACHERS MAKE BETTER INSTRUCTIONAL DECISIONS

CREATING & USING LEARNING TARGETS & PERFORMANCE SCALES

HOW TEACHERS MAKE BETTER INSTRUCTIONAL DECISIONS

Carla Moore
Libby H. Garst
Robert J. Marzano

With Elizabeth Kennedy and Deana Senn

Learning Sciences
MARZANO
C E N T E R

1400 Centrepark Blvd, Suite 1000
West Palm Beach, FL 33401
717-845-6300

email: pub@learningsciences.com
learningsciences.com

Printed in the United States of America

20 19 18 17 16 15   2 3 4

Publisher's Cataloging-in-Publication Data

Moore, Carla.
  Creating & using learning targets & performance scales: how teachers make better instructional decisions / Carla Moore, Libby H. Garst, [and] Robert J. Marzano.
     pages cm. – (Essentials for achieving rigor series)
  ISBN: 978-1-941112-01-4 (pbk.)
1. Student-centered learning. 2. Students—Self-rating of. 3. Effective teach-ing—United States. 4. Academic achievement. 5. Learning, Psychology of. I. Moore, Carla. II. Marzano, Robert J. III. Title.
  LB1025.3 .M3385 2014
  370.15`23—dc23
                    [2014939913]

MARZANO CENTER

Essentials for Achieving Rigor SERIES

The *Essentials for Achieving Rigor* series of instructional guides helps educators become highly skilled at implementing, monitoring, and adapting instruction. Put it to practical use immediately, adopting day-to-day examples as models for application in your own classroom.

Books in the series:

Identifying Critical Content: Classroom Techniques to Help Students Know What Is Important

Examining Reasoning: Classroom Techniques to Help Students Produce and Defend Claims

Recording & Representing Knowledge: Classroom Techniques to Help Students Accurately Organize and Summarize Content

Examining Similarities & Differences: Classroom Techniques to Help Students Deepen Their Understanding

Processing New Information: Classroom Techniques to Help Students Engage With Content

Revising Knowledge: Classroom Techniques to Help Students Examine Their Deeper Understanding

Practicing Skills, Strategies & Processes: Classroom Techniques to Help Students Develop Proficiency

Engaging in Cognitively Complex Tasks: Classroom Techniques to Help Students Generate & Test Hypotheses Across Disciplines

Creating & Using Learning Targets & Performance Scales: How Teachers Make Better Instructional Decisions

Organizing for Learning: Classroom Techniques to Help Students Interact Within Small Groups

Dedication

I dedicate this work to my first educators, Mom and Dad, and to Gary, Erica, and Will, who continue to teach and inspire me daily.

—Carla Moore

I dedicate this work to my children, Bradley and Alyson, whose academic peaks and valleys inspired me to be a better educator.

—Libby H. Garst

Table of Contents

Acknowledgments

Learning Sciences International would like to thank the following reviewers:

George E. Goodfellow
2008 Rhode Island State Teacher of
  the Year
Scituate High School
North Scituate, Rhode Island

Aaron Sitze
2013 Illinois Teacher of the Year
  finalist
Oregon High School
Oregon, Illinois

Robin L. Oliveri
2014 Leon County Schools Teacher
  of the Year
Godby High School
Tallahassee, Florida

Lisa Staats
2012 North Carolina Teacher of the
  Year finalist
Chocowinity Middle School
Chocowinity, North Carolina

About the Authors

CARLA MOORE, MSEd, is an experienced professional developer, teacher, and administrator who oversees content and product development for Learning Sciences International, with a special emphasis on teacher and administrator effectiveness. For more than a decade, she was a member of district-based professional development where she served in many roles, including director of quality instruction at St. Lucie County Public Schools in Florida. She co-led the implementation of the Marzano Teacher Evaluation Model and supported training within the district to meet strategic milestones for student achievement. She is nationally recognized for her commitment to K–12 education, having received the 2013 Florida Association of Staff Development Award, a Schlechty Centre Conference Fellowship, and the Treasure Coast News Lifetime Achiever of Education Award, among others. In addition, she challenges audiences at state and national forums to continuously grow in the area of pedagogical excellence. Carla and her loving husband, Gary, enjoy the South Florida life with their two children, Erica and Will.

LIBBY H. GARST, MSEd, creates professional development for teacher growth as a staff developer and instructional designer for the Learning Sciences International Marzano Center. She has written numerous resources on research-based instructional strategies for Learning Sciences International's iObservation library and facilitated online courses for the Art and Science of Teaching master of science program for the National Institute for Professional Practice. Libby has been a successful teacher and instructional coach at both the elementary and middle school levels. She is a graduate of Virginia Tech and received her master's degree from the University of Virginia. Libby is married to Wesley, her devoted husband, and has two talented children, Bradley and Alyson.

 **ROBERT J. MARZANO, PhD,** is CEO of Marzano Research Laboratory and executive director of the Learning Sciences International Marzano Center for Teacher and Leader Evaluation. A leading researcher in education, he is a speaker, trainer, and author of more than 150 articles on topics such as instruction, assessment, writing and implementing standards, cognition, effective leadership, and school intervention. He has authored over 30 books, including *The Art and Science of Teaching* (ASCD, 2007) and *Teacher Evaluation That Makes a Difference* (ASCD, 2013).

ELIZABETH A. KENNEDY, MEd, directs and implements Learning Sciences International's pilot research projects in schools and districts. She brings 39 years of successful experience as a public school teacher and school administrator at both the elementary and middle school levels.

DEANA SENN, MSSE, is the lead content developer and a senior staff developer for the Learning Sciences International Marzano Center. Her experience spans the United States and Canada in both rural and urban settings. Deana received her bachelor's degree from Texas A&M University and master's degree from Montana State University.

Introduction

This guide, *Creating & Using Learning Targets & Performance Scales: How Teachers Make Better Instructional Decisions,* is intended as a resource for improving a specific aspect of instructional practice: creating and using learning targets and performance scales.

Your motivation to incorporate this strategy into your instructional tool-box may have come from a personal desire to improve your instructional practice through the implementation of a research-based set of strategies (such as those found in the Marzano instructional framework) or a desire to increase the rigor of the instructional strategies you implement in your class-room so that students meet the expectations of demanding standards such as the Common Core State Standards, Next Generation Science Standards, C3 Framework for Social Studies State Standards, or state standards based on or influenced by College and Career Readiness Anchor Standards.

This guide will help teachers of all grade levels and subjects improve their performance of a specific instructional strategy: creating and using learning targets and performance scales. Narrowing your focus on a specific skill, such as creating and using learning targets and performance scales, permits you to concentrate on the nuances of this instructional strategy to deliberately improve it. This allows you to intentionally plan, implement, monitor, adapt, and reflect on this single element of your instructional practice. A person seeking to become an expert displays distinctive behaviors, as explained by Marzano and Toth (2013):

- breaks down the specific skills required to be an expert

- focuses on improving those particular critical skill chunks (as opposed to easy tasks) during practice or day-to-day activities

- receives immediate, specific, and actionable feedback, particularly from a more experienced coach

- continually practices each critical skill at more challenging levels with the intention of mastering it, giving far less time to skills already mastered

This series of guides will support each of the previously listed behaviors, with a focus on breaking down the specific skills required to be an expert and giving day-to-day practical suggestions to enhance these skills.

Building on the Marzano Instructional Model

This series is based on the Marzano instructional framework, which is grounded in research and provides educators with the tools they need to connect instructional practice to student achievement. The series uses key terms that are specific to the Marzano model of instruction. See Table 1, Glossary of Key Terms.

Table 1: Glossary of Key Terms

Term	Definition
CCSS	Common Core State Standards is the official name of the standards documents developed by the Common Core State Standards Initiative (CCSSI), the goal of which is to prepare students in the United States for college and career.
CCR	College and Career Readiness Anchor Standards are broad statements that incorporate individual standards for various grade levels and specific content areas.
Desired result	The intended result for the student(s) due to the implementation of a specific strategy.
Monitoring	The act of checking for evidence of the desired result of a specific strategy while the strategy is being implemented.
Instructional strategy	A category of techniques used for classroom instruction that has been proven to have a high probability of enhancing student achievement.
Instructional technique	The method used to teach and deepen understanding of knowledge and skills.
Content	The knowledge and skills necessary for students to demonstrate standards.
Scaffolding	A purposeful progression of support that targets cognitive complexity and student autonomy to reach rigor.
Extending	Activities that move students who have already demonstrated the desired result to a higher level of understanding.

The educational pendulum swings widely from decade to decade. Educators move back and forth between prescriptive checklists and step-by-step lesson plans to approaches that encourage instructional autonomy with minimal regard for the science of teaching and need for accountability. Two practices are often missing in both of these approaches to defining effective instruction: 1) specific statements of desired results and 2) solid research-based connections. The Marzano instructional framework provides a comprehensive system that details what is required from teachers to develop their craft using research-based instructional strategies. Launching from this solid instructional foundation, teachers will then be prepared to merge that science with their own unique, yet effective, instructional style, which is the art of teaching.

Creating & Using Learning Targets and Performance Scales: How Teachers Make Better Instructional Decisions will help you grow into an innovative and highly skilled teacher who is able to implement, scaffold, and extend instruction to meet a range of student needs.

Essentials for Achieving Rigor

This series of guides details essential classroom strategies to support the complex shifts in teaching that are necessary for an environment where academic rigor is a requirement for all students. The instructional strategies presented in this series are essential to effectively teach the CCSS, the Next Generation Science Standards, or standards designated by your school district or state. They require a deeper understanding of content, more effective use of strategies, and greater frequency of implementation for your students to demonstrate the knowledge and skills required by rigorous standards. This series includes instructional techniques appropriate for all grade levels and content areas. The examples contained within are grade-level specific and should serve as models and launching points for application in your own classroom.

Your skillful implementation of these strategies is essential to your students' mastery of the CCSS or other rigorous standards, no matter the grade level or subject you are teaching. Other instructional strategies covered in the Essentials for Achieving Rigor series, such as examining reasoning and engaging students in cognitively complex tasks, exemplify the cognitive complexity needed to meet rigorous standards. Taken as a package, these strategies may at first glance seem quite daunting. For this reason, the series focuses on just one strategy in each guide.

Creating and Using Learning Targets and Performance Scales

If you have read and used other guides in the Essentials for Achieving Rigor series, you are accustomed to immediately finding a set of techniques to help you become more proficient in using a specific instructional strategy. In this guide, however, the content is organized somewhat differently.

In the other guides in the series, the techniques to help you teach the specific content of your grade or discipline are featured front and center, based on the assumption that you already have the content of your grade or discipline well in hand. However, absent the learning targets and performance scales described in this guide, you and your students may well lack a clear direction for learning.

Your hard work, as well as the efforts of your students, can easily become time expended on the wrong content. To effectively implement this strategy, you must first acquire the skills and knowledge needed to *create* learning targets and performance scales. Once the creation process is mastered, you can readily *implement* the targets and scales for any content at any grade level.

To show you how to both create and implement learning targets and performance scales, this guide is divided into two parts. Part I introduces you to the knowledge and skills needed to create learning targets and performance scales. You will learn a step-by-step process for creating your own targets and scales using the following steps: 1) unpack standards to identify learning targets, 2) use a taxonomy to identify levels of cognitive complexity required by the standards, and 3) organize targets into a scale that describes levels of performance. Once you have acquired the necessary knowledge and skills to create your own targets and scales, you will be shown how to use them in your classroom in Part II. The second part of the guide introduces four techniques to help you effectively implement learning targets and performance scales: 1) routines for using targets and scales, 2) using teacher-created targets and scales, 3) using student-friendly scales, and 4) using student-generated scales.

PART I

CREATING LEARNING TARGETS AND PERFORMANCE SCALES

Learning targets and performance scales are tools that can help you become more efficient and effective in designing and delivering instruction. These tools will help both you and your students focus on the progression of instruction through lessons and units. In the beginning, the process may seem cumbersome, but like any type of procedural knowledge, practice will soon produce fluency.

The creation of learning targets and performance scales begins with understanding how these tools can help you delineate and communicate the essential declarative and procedural knowledge you want students to master. You will encounter a variety of terms related to the creation of targets and scales as you read. They are defined and explained in Table 2. At first glance, the terms may seem confusing. However, as you learn the various steps involved in creating targets and scales in Part I, you will soon acquire the deeper understandings you need to move forward into implementation.

Table 2: Glossary of Terms Related to Creation of Learning Targets and Performance Scales

Term	Definition
Procedural knowledge	Skills or processes that students will be able to perform that demonstrate understanding of the content being addressed.
Declarative knowledge	Informational knowledge that students will understand in regard to the content being addressed.
Basic processes	Fundamental practices or competencies that supply the experiences necessary to attain an ability or skill.
Academic standard	A statement generated at the national, state, or local level that designates the approved educational benchmarks and conveys what students are expected to learn at a specified grade level and content area.
Learning goal	The educational objective that describes what students will understand and be able to perform in regard to the content being addressed. An effective learning goal is composed of clearly stated *learning targets* that demonstrate attainment and mastery performance of the academic standard.
Cognitively complex targets	Learning targets that contain the level of processing or cognitive complexity beyond the requirements of the academic standard.
Foundational targets	Learning targets that contain essential prerequisites, knowledge, and basic processes not explicitly stated in an academic standard, but necessary to construct the initial understandings required to reach the learning goal target. The levels of thinking required by foundational targets are below the levels of processing or cognitive complexity required by the standard and learning goal targets.
Learning goal targets	Learning targets at the same level of cognitive complexity as the academic standard that identify the skills required to demonstrate mastery of the content.
Learning targets	Generic targets made up of short descriptive phrases typically bulleted or outlined in a performance scale that detail the knowledge and skills students must understand and be able to perform to demonstrate understanding of an academic standard.
Performance scale	A continuum that articulates distinct levels of knowledge and skills relative to a specific standard.

The information contained in the various types of targets in Table 2 is derived from the essential knowledge, skills, and processes embedded in standards. Once you have identified the various learning targets that emerge as you unpack a standard, you will be able to create a performance scale.

A performance scale organizes the various types of targets on a continuum that ranges from simpler to more complex thinking. A well-designed scale, based on the identified targets, functions as a communication tool between you and your students as it outlines the progression of learning toward the learning goal. Performance scales are composed of individual learning targets that work together and gradually build toward mastery of a specific academic standard. As you teach critical content to students, plan to refer to the pertinent aspects of a specific performance scale in both timely and consistent ways. Performance scales provide both you and your students with the incremental steps or expectations toward the mastery of the standard.

Creating Learning Targets

Learning targets provide a focus for planning and enable you to work more efficiently. These targets not only serve as communication tools that set forth the criteria for student success in each lesson but also function as feedback tools that provide information to you and your students about their performance. Learning targets drive what is taught, to include all activities, assignments, and assessments that occur during the course of lessons or units. The benefits of learning targets extend beyond the classroom for teachers as they facilitate communication between colleagues, coaches, and school leaders and provide a focus for their collaborative work in professional learning communities.

For students, learning targets provide an accurate guide to what they need to learn on a day-to-day basis. Learning targets establish the clear criteria for what the students need to demonstrate to successfully meet the expectations for each lesson and ultimately attain the academic standard. When students grasp their learning targets, they often become empowered to take ownership and responsibility for future learning.

Learning targets compel all stakeholders to be aligned across similar grade levels and subject matter, and they should be articulated with colleagues above and below the stakeholders. When colleagues are working toward the same learning targets, the goal of supporting students and helping them meet the established learning expectations becomes easier to achieve. Learning targets help focus conversations between the teacher and the students, requiring everyone to concentrate on what he or she is supposed to learn, not just on the completion of an activity or assignment. Learning targets also benefit parents and other family members by keeping them informed of the expectations for their students.

After reading about these various benefits of learning targets, you might conclude that once you have learned how to create them, you will be ready to plan lessons and activities for tomorrow. However, keep in mind as you gain background knowledge and skills for creating learning targets in the following section that the creation of learning targets is not your end product. Learning targets are designed in the service of creating performance scales.

How to Effectively Create Learning Targets

The following section describes how to effectively create learning targets and is divided into two parts: 1) background knowledge you need to create learning targets and 2) a step-by-step tutorial for creating those targets.

Background Knowledge

In anticipation of learning how to create effective learning targets, you will need to thoroughly understand two bodies of information: 1) the differences between the two types of knowledge in the standards and 2) the critical attributes of three types of learning targets. This background knowledge will provide you with the conceptual understanding needed to create learning targets.

Declarative and Procedural Knowledge

Declarative knowledge will usually be situated in the *nouns* of a standard. The nouns represent information, such as vocabulary terms, facts, time sequences, generalizations, or principles, that are essential for students to build upon as they attain more complex skills. For example, the CCSS ELA standard RL 7.6 asks students to *analyze how an author develops characters and contrasts the point of view of different characters or narrators in a text*. A teacher might ask, "What do I have to teach my students so they are able to analyze a text?" Before students can analyze character development, they must understand what the terms *point of view, characters,* and *narrators* mean. Building declarative knowledge lays a foundation for more complex content. Students will often need multiple exposures to the concepts through varied activities that allow them to systematically review their initial understanding of content and deepen that knowledge. This declarative knowledge must be developed before students can gain the fluency or the increased level of controlled processing necessary to move on to the procedural knowledge, which in the case of the previously mentioned standard is the process of text analysis.

Procedural knowledge involves skills, strategies, and processes. The indicators of procedural knowledge encompassed in state and national standards are usually situated in the verbs. In the previous example, the verbs *analyze* and *contrast* provide clues for how to develop learning targets. Teaching procedural knowledge requires modeling the skill, guided practice, feedback and correction of errors or misunderstandings, and various types of practice until students have developed the automaticity necessary to independently apply the procedural knowledge in varied contexts.

Three Types of Learning Targets

There are three types of learning targets: 1) learning goal targets, 2) foundational targets, and 3) cognitively complex targets. In the following sections, they are defined in detail.

Learning Goal Targets. Learning goal targets are statements of the knowledge and skills students need to demonstrate mastery of a standard. They are derived directly from state or national academic standards and identify what students should know and be able to do by the end of a grade or course. Unpacking individual standards will provide the information needed to create daily or weekly learning targets that include the content focus, cognitive level of thinking, and precise language necessary to delineate learning goal targets. Remember that learning goal targets require the same level of cognitive complexity as the standard and often require a series of lessons to accomplish. To determine a logical learning progression, first identify what the standard is asking students to know (declarative knowledge) and demonstrate (procedural knowledge) to master the standard.

Foundational Targets. Foundational targets consist of knowledge and basic processes that build to the cognitive level of the academic standard. They constitute the prerequisites that students need to master to ultimately achieve the learning goal targets. There are two types of foundational targets: 1) those that identify declarative knowledge and 2) those that identify procedural knowledge.

Foundational Targets for Declarative Knowledge. Foundational targets for declarative knowledge identify the academic vocabulary that is essential for learning the standard. To identify the essential academic vocabulary to be targeted, ask the following questions:

- Do students need to know the word or term to demonstrate an understanding of the standard?

- Did students learn this word or term in a previous grade or class?

If the answer to the first question is yes, the term should be considered a potential vocabulary word to be targeted. However, if the answer to the second question is also yes, unless the term is being used in a different capacity from how it was used in previous grades or classes, it should not be a target. The term might need to be reviewed and discussed at some point, but it is not considered new knowledge and therefore should not be considered a foundational target.

Foundational Targets for Procedural Knowledge. Foundational targets also include any basic skills or processes students must perform to attain the learning goal target. These are the processes or skills that provide the underpinning for future targets and must be achieved before students can be successful with the current learning goal target. Ask the following questions to identify the essential skills or processes that need to be targeted:

- What do students need to be able to do before they can meet the learning goal target?

- Did students learn this skill or process in a previous grade or class?

After answering the first question and listing the foundational skills and processes required, consider the answer to the second question. Just as with the vocabulary, if the answer to the second question is yes, then students may need a brief review of previous skills and processes. However, do not consider these prerequisite skills to be foundational targets. Unless the skill is being presented or used in a different capacity, it is not considered new. Only new skills required to build toward the cognitive complexity of the learning goal target should be categorized as foundational targets.

Cognitively Complex Targets. These targets are created to help students extend and deepen the knowledge and skills of the standard. The expectations in these targets are more rigorous than the learning goal targets in a standard. This category of learning targets requires deeper thinking than the standard requires and expects that students will think about the same content in more complex ways. In other words, cognitively complex targets ask students to use the knowledge and skills of the standard to extend their thinking and make applications beyond what is set forth in the standard.

Creating Learning Targets

You are no doubt eager to begin creating learning targets for your students. The following tutorial is divided into two parts: 1) organizational tasks and decisions that must be made in advance of the actual hands-on work of creating the targets and 2) a step-by-step process that will enable you to create a learning target.

Organizational Tasks and Decisions

There are several organizational tasks and decisions that need to be made in advance of creating learning targets. These activities can take place either at the district office, in school teams, or in professional learning communities and include the following: 1) identifying the essential standards for grade levels or content specialties, 2) grouping these standards into units to be taught over a school year, 3) agreeing on the intent or embedded purpose of each standard, and 4) clarifying for all stakeholders the scope of the standards relative to how they build on previous learning and ultimately prepare students for academic success in subsequent grades or courses. Once these organizational activities are completed, you and your colleagues will be ready to create learning targets.

A Step-by-Step Process for Creating Learning Targets

There are four steps in the process of creating learning targets: 1) identify the declarative and procedural knowledge of the standard, 2) chunk the standard, 3) unpack the foundational targets, and 4) create cognitively complex targets.

Step 1: Identify the Declarative and Procedural Knowledge in a Standard.
The first step in the creation of learning targets is to identify the declarative and procedural knowledge of the standard. In the typical standard, the procedural knowledge is found in the verbs, while the declarative knowledge is found in the nouns. Three examples (Figures A, B, and C)—one from each grade span (K–5, 6–8, and 9–12)—illustrate this step. Carefully work your way through the three examples, noting that the verbs (procedural knowledge) are circled and the nouns (declarative knowledge) are underlined. When you are working with a selected standard from your grade level or discipline, circle the verbs and underline the nouns. Although these examples may not illustrate the specific grade level or content you teach, the process is identical for any subject or grade level. Figure A displays an elementary example of identifying declarative and procedural knowledge.

Figure A: Elementary Example of Identifying Declarative and Procedural Knowledge

Elementary – English Language Arts   Grade: Kindergarten

(CCSS.ELA-Literacy.RL.K.3): With prompting and support, identify characters, settings, and major events in a story.

(CCSS.ELA-Literacy.RL.K.1): With prompting and support, ask and answer questions about key details in a text.

Figure B shows a middle school math example in which the verbs (procedural knowledge) are circled and the nouns (declarative knowledge) are underlined in two middle school standards.

Figure B: Middle School Example of Identifying Declarative and Procedural Knowledge

---

Middle School – Mathematics   Grade: Eighth

(CCSS.Math.8.NS.A.1): Know that numbers that are not rational are called irrational. Understand informally that every number has a decimal expansion; for rational numbers show that the decimal expansion repeats eventually and convert a decimal expansion which repeats eventually into a rational number.

(CCSS.Math.8.NS.A.2): Use rational approximations of irrational numbers to compare the size of irrational numbers, locate them approximately on a number line diagram, and estimate the value of expressions (e.g., π^2).

Figure C is a high school example identifying declarative and procedural knowledge from several high school biology standards.

Figure C: High School Example of Identifying Declarative and Procedural Knowledge

---

High School – Biology   Grades: Ninth–Twelfth

(CPALMS: Life Science SC.912.L.14.2): Relate structure to function for the components of plant and animal cells. Explain the role of cell membranes as a highly selective barrier (passive and active transport).

(CPALMS: Life Science SC.912.L.14.3): Compare and contrast the general structures of plant and animal cells. Compare and contrast the general structures of prokaryotic cells and eukaryotic cells.

(CPALMS: Life Science SC.912.L.14.4): Compare and contrast structure and function of various types of microscopes.

Step 2: Chunk the Standard. Chunking a standard means breaking it apart into chunks called learning goal targets. Chunking is not difficult, but the process requires a careful reading of the action verbs and a word-by-word conversion of the sentences and paragraphs in the standards into bulleted learning goal targets.

Figure D illustrates how the kindergarten English language arts standards have been transformed into five individual learning goal targets. The circled verbs from the examples in step 1 appear in bold type wherever they occur. Notice how the single standard containing a series of nouns following a verb has been unpacked into several learning targets. Note the phrase that precedes each of the learning goal targets: *students will be able to.*

Figure D: Learning Goal Targets for Kindergarten English Language Arts

Elementary – English Language Arts	Grade: Kindergarten
(CCSS.ELA-Literacy.RL.K.3): With prompting and support, **identify** characters, settings, and major events in a story.	
(CCSS.Math.8.NS.A.2): With prompting and support, **ask** and **answer** questions about key details in a text.	

Learning Goal Targets Students will be able to:
• **Identify** characters in a story • **Identify** settings in a story • **Identify** major events in a story • **Ask** questions about key details in a text • **Answer** questions about key details in a text

Figure E shows how the essential knowledge and skills of two middle school math standards have been chunked into seven individual learning goal targets. The process of creating learning goal targets, whether executed by you individually or with your colleagues, will help you focus your lesson planning and assessments more directly and give students more discrete learning targets during lessons and units.

Figure E: Learning Goal Targets for Middle School Mathematics

Middle School – Mathematics	Grade: Eighth

(CCSS.Math.8.NS.A.1): Know that numbers that are not rational are called irrational. **Understand** informally that every number has a decimal expansion; for rational numbers **show** that the decimal expansion **repeats** eventually, and **convert** a decimal expansion which **repeats** eventually into a rational number.

(CCSS.Math.8.NS.A.2): Use rational approximations of irrational numbers to **compare** the size of irrational numbers, **locate** them approximately on a number line diagram, and **estimate** the value of expressions (e.g., π^2).

Learning Goal Targets
Students will be able to:

- **Know** that numbers that are not rational are called irrational
- **Understand** informally that every number has a decimal expansion
- **Show** that the decimal expansion repeats eventually for rational numbers
- **Convert** a decimal expansion which repeats eventually into a rational number
- **Use** rational approximations of irrational numbers to compare the size of irrational numbers
- **Locate** irrational numbers approximately on a number line diagram
- **Estimate** the value of expressions (e.g., π^2)

Figure F illustrates how three high school biology standards have been chunked into five learning goal targets.

Figure F: Learning Goal Targets for High School Biology

High School – Biology	Grades: Ninth–Twelfth

(CPALMS: Life Science SC.912.L.14.2): Relate structure to function for the components of plant and animal cells. **Explain** the role of cell membranes as a highly selective barrier (passive and active transport).

(CPALMS: Life Science SC.912.L.14.3): Compare and **contrast** the general structures of plant and animal cells. **Compare** and **contrast** the general structures of prokaryotic and eukaryotic cells.

(CPALMS: Life Science SC.912.L.14.4): Compare and **contrast** structure and function of various types of microscopes.

Learning Goal Targets
Students will be able to:

- **Relate** structure to function for the components of plant and animal cells
- **Explain** the role of cell membranes as a highly selective barrier (passive and active transport)
- **Compare** and **contrast** the general structures of plant and animal cells
- **Compare** and **contrast** the general structures of prokaryotic and eukaryotic cells
- **Compare** and **contrast** structure and function of various types of microscopes

Step 3: Unpack the Foundational Targets. In the previous step, you transformed an academic standard into a set of discrete learning goal targets based on the verbs you circled in the standard. In a sense, the highlighted verbs seem to provide you with a quick to-do list for you and your students. However, do not conclude that you now have all the information you need to begin planning your lessons. In this step, you must reconceptualize or reframe those discrete learning goal targets by unpacking them into still another set of targets known as foundational targets.

Foundational targets contain prerequisite knowledge and processes not always explicitly stated in the academic standard. Unpacking the foundational targets will reveal the prerequisite understandings students need to have mastered to attain the learning goal targets of the standards. Note that the thinking levels of the foundational targets are less cognitively complex than the thinking levels that the standard and its learning goal targets require.

To create the foundational targets, the declarative knowledge, or nouns, from the standard are unpacked to reveal all of the vocabulary, key concepts, and basic processes students need to know and do to attain the learning goal targets. Three examples in Figures G, H, and I demonstrate how foundational targets have been created for the previously identified standards. Note that the first row restates the standards, a constant reminder to retain your focus on the intent and scope of each standard.

As you read through the three sets of foundational processes in the following examples, notice that the targets that have been reconceptualized as foundational processes are the identical targets that were labeled learning goal targets in the previous step. Recall the earlier statement you read: Learning targets are created in the service of creating performance scales. The questions you have about this step in creating targets will be answered when you learn how to create performance scales.

Figure G displays the two types of knowledge in foundational targets. The declarative knowledge is in the left-hand column, now conceptualized as foundational knowledge, and the procedural knowledge is in the right-hand column, now conceptualized as foundational processes. Foundational targets constitute both prerequisite knowledge your students must understand and prerequisite processes your students must be able to execute.

Figure G: Foundational Targets for Kindergarten English Language Arts

Elementary – English Language Arts	Grade: Kindergarten

(CCSS.ELA-Literacy.RL.K.3): With prompting and support, **identify** characters, settings, and major events in a story.

(CCSS.ELA-Literacy.RL.K.1): With prompting and support, **ask** and **answer** questions about key details in a text.

Foundational Knowledge Students will understand:	Foundational Processes Students will be able to:
• Vocabulary: *story, setting, characters, events, ask, answer, detail, question, text* • Characters in a story • Settings in a story • Major events in a story	• **Identify** characters in a story • **Identify** settings in a story • **Identify** major events in a story • **Ask** questions about key details in a text • **Answer** questions about key details in a text

Figure H shows the foundational targets for middle school math. Notice as in earlier figures, the verbs are in bold print to bring them to the forefront of your thinking as you create the foundational targets.

Figure H: Foundational Targets for Middle School Mathematics

Middle School – Mathematics	Grade: Eighth

(CCSS.Math.8.NS.A.1): Know that numbers that are not rational are called irrational. **Understand** informally that every number has a decimal expansion; for rational numbers **show** that the decimal expansion **repeats** eventually, and **convert** a decimal expansion which **repeats** eventually into a rational number.

(CCSS.Math.8.NS.A.2): Use rational approximations of irrational numbers to **compare** the size of irrational numbers, **locate** them approximately on a number line diagram, and **estimate** the value of expressions (e.g., π^2).

Foundational Knowledge Students will understand:	Foundational Processes Students will be able to:
• Vocabulary: *rational numbers, irrational numbers, decimal expansion, convert, nonrepeating decimal, nonterminating decimal* • Numbers that are not rational are irrational • Every number has a decimal expansion • Decimal expansion repeats eventually in rational numbers • Rational approximations can be made for irrational numbers and can be used to compare and estimate value • Irrational numbers can be located on a number line diagram	• **Know** that numbers that are not rational are called irrational • **Understand** informally that every number has a decimal expansion • **Show** that the decimal expansion repeats eventually for rational numbers • **Convert** a decimal expansion which repeats eventually into a rational number • **Use** rational approximations of irrational numbers to **compare** the size of irrational numbers • **Locate** irrational numbers on a number line diagram • **Estimate** the value of irrational expressions (e.g., π^2)

Figure I displays the foundational knowledge and processes unpacked from three high school biology standards.

Figure I: Foundational Targets for High School Biology

High School – Biology	Grades: Ninth–Twelfth

(CPALMS: Life Science SC.912.L.14.2): Relate structure to function for the components of plant and animal cells. **Explain** the role of cell membranes as a highly selective barrier (passive and active transport).

(CPALMS: Life Science SC.912.L.14.3): Compare and **contrast** the general structures of plant and animal cells. Compare and contrast the general structures of prokaryotic and eukaryotic cells.

(CPALMS: Life Science SC.912.L.14.4): Compare and **contrast** structure and function of various types of microscopes.

Foundational Knowledge Students will understand:	Foundational Processes Students will be able to:
• Vocabulary: *plant cells, animal cells, eukaryotic cells, cell membrane (plasma membrane), highly selective barrier, permeable, active transport, passive transport, cell wall, cytoplasm, ribosomes, nucleus, nuclear membrane, nucleolus, chromatic, endoplasmic reticulum, microtubules, microfilaments, vacuoles, mitochondria, Golgi apparatus, chloroplasts, lysosomes, hypotonic, hypertonic, isotonic solutions, component, organelle, chromosomes, phospholipid, polar, molecule, vesicles* • Components of a eukaryotic cell • Structures and functions of the components of plant and animal cells • Cell membrane is highly selective barrier • Materials pass in and out of a cell	• **Relate** structure to function for the components of plant and animal cells • **Explain** the role of cell membranes as a highly selective barrier (passive and active transport) • **Compare** and **contrast** the general structure of plant and animal cells • **Compare** and **contrast** the general structures of prokaryotic and eukaryotic cells • **Compare** and **contrast** structure and function of various types of microscopes

Step 4: Create Cognitively Complex Targets. Cognitively complex targets are learning targets that require a level of processing or cognitive complexity that compels students to delve more deeply into the content of the academic standard. Creating this type of target may seem somewhat intimidating at first. However, the easiest way is to carefully consider your selected standard, and then think of some different ways that this standard might be authentically used in the real world. Contemplate how you might ask your students to use the knowledge and skills gained from the learning goal targets to delve deeper into the content and extend their learning. See the examples in Figures J, K, and L, and note how these targets require students to engage at

higher thinking levels than do the actual standards. The derivation of those targets is less obvious. Only the target in Figure L seems to have been generated by focusing on a real-world application as suggested earlier. If you are wondering how, for example, the cognitively complex target in Figure J was derived from the set of English language arts standards or the target in the middle school math standards in Figure K, you are definitely ready to move on to the creation of performance scales. There you will explore the creation of cognitively complex targets in more depth as you learn how to create performance scales using Marzano's Taxonomy of educational objectives (Marzano & Brown, 2009). There is a method, so hold your question. The solution lies in the relationship of the performance scale levels to various taxonomy levels.

Figure J displays a cognitively complex target generated from the two kindergarten English language arts standards. While you may not be certain of precisely where the terms *compare* and *contrast* came from, you can no doubt readily accept that they will be more cognitively challenging tasks for five-year-olds than merely identifying characters or asking and answering questions.

Figure J: Cognitively Complex Targets for Kindergarten English Language Arts

Standard	Cognitively Complex Targets
(CCSS.ELA-Literacy.RL.K.3): With prompting and support, **identify** characters, settings, and major events in a story. **(CCSS.ELA-Literacy.RL.K.1):** With prompting and support, **ask** and **answer** questions about key details in a text.	• Compare and contrast key details of a story, including characters, settings, and major events.

Figure K displays a cognitively complex target for a middle school math standard. Once again, take a moment to acknowledge the increased cognitive complexity of evaluating as compared to knowing, understanding, showing, and converting.

Figure K: Cognitively Complex Targets for Middle School Mathematics

Standard	Cognitively Complex Targets
(CCSS.Math.8.NS.A.1): Know that numbers that are not rational are called irrational. **Understand** informally that every number has a decimal expansion; for rational numbers **show** that the decimal expansion repeats eventually, and **convert** a decimal expansion which repeats eventually into a rational number. **(CCSS.Math.8.NS.A.2): Use** rational approximations of irrational numbers to **compare** the size of irrational numbers, **locate** them approximately on a number line diagram, and **estimate** the value of expressions (e.g., π^2).	• Investigate the outcome of applying properties (addition, subtraction, multiplication, division) to both rational and irrational numbers.

Figure L shows a cognitively complex target that expects students to use the knowledge and skills from the standard in integrative and investigative ways.

Figure L: Cognitively Complex Targets for High School Biology

Standard	Cognitively Complex Targets
(CPALMS Life Science SC.912.L.14.2): Relate structure to function for the components of plant and animal cells. **Explain** the role of cell membranes as a highly selective barrier (passive and active transport). **(CPALMS Life Science SC.912.L.14.3): Compare** and **contrast** the general structures of plant and animal cells. **Compare** and **contrast** the general structures of prokaryotic and eukaryotic cells. **(CPALMS Life Science SC.912.L.14.4): Compare** and **contrast** structure and function of various types of microscopes.	• Research ways that cell components are used in medical advancement.

Learning how to create learning targets will assuredly take an investment of your time. However, if you collaborate with your grade-level team or department, the process can be completed more quickly as you work together to discover the intent of the standard. You can continue the discussion of how the standard will look in the classroom, and then follow through with the process for creating targets. Activities and discussions of this nature will cultivate a common understanding and language around instruction. More important, however, the learning targets you create will become the components of the performance scales you create in the following section.

Creating Performance Scales

Now that you have gained familiarity with the three types of learning targets and are able to create them for the standards your students need to master, you are ready to organize those targets into performance scales. A performance scale is a continuum that articulates distinct levels of knowledge and skills relative to specific standards. When used as intended, performance scales will drive lessons, activities, assignments, and assessments. If you prefer a low-tech metaphor for understanding a performance scale, think of it as a road map to guide you through a set of lessons or units of instruction. If you are more disposed to high-tech metaphors, imagine a performance scale as an educational GPS, guiding you and your students—letting you know where you are in the journey, how much farther you must travel to reach your destination, and what lies ahead. If you inadvertently make a wrong turn on your learning journey, a performance scale can alert you and your students about the need to recalculate or make a legal U-turn. Performance scales articulate distinct levels of knowledge and skills relative to achieving the standard and, once organized according to their appropriate taxonomy levels, become a progression of learning that guides your journey.

Performance scales organize learning targets into highly useful structures and make teaching visible to students. "When learner goals have been articulated in scale format, the teacher and students have clear direction about instructional targets as well as descriptions of levels of understanding and performance for those targets" (Marzano, 2007, p. 23). Well-constructed scales help you work more efficiently to cover the content, because the learning targets are organized into a sequence of lessons. When faithfully implemented, a well-constructed scale also enables you to be more selective about the activities and tasks you assign, disqualifying any that are not aligned to the standard. Performance scales also can serve as a conduit for feedback because they help the teacher concentrate and provide direct responses on individual or class performance. While a scale and its targets may take some time to create, they actually save time overall, as you can more efficiently focus your planning, instruction, and assessment.

All students will benefit from the clear learning path embedded in a well-constructed performance scale. Students who previously lagged behind will begin to make connections between the tasks, activities, and assessments they are completing in class each day, thereby pointing them to a specific learning goal. When scales are used as a tool for providing feedback, students know their current level of performance and what they specifically need to do to continue advancing toward the learning target. Students also share in the challenge of learning, adopt self-assessment and evaluation strategies, develop error detection strategies, and experience heightened levels of self-efficacy necessary to tackle more challenging tasks that lead to mastery and deeper understanding of the content.

For students to receive the learning benefits from using performance scales, you need to be certain of the learning destination and specifically aware of how each assignment, task, and assessment will lead students toward the learning goal. The standards-based classroom should be structured such that every task is aligned to a learning target that guides students to mastery of the standards. Both you and your students must be aware of the alignment. A shift to that level of awareness does not happen quickly, but it is a shift that is worth bringing to your classroom and your colleagues' classrooms.

How to Create Performance Scales

The foundation for creating performance scales was laid in the previous section when you learned how to create three levels of learning targets: 1) foundational targets, 2) learning goal targets, and 3) cognitively complex targets. Knowledge and skills were identified from a specified standard that in turn created actionable chunks of content. At this point, you are ready to organize your targets into a performance scale. As needed during your creation of performance scales, review the definitions of the various types of targets in Table 2 (page 8). In addition, gather the three sets of learning targets you may have already developed for a specific standard. You will refer to them frequently as you create your performance scale. This tutorial for creating performance scales is divided into two parts: 1) satisfying the prerequisites for creating performance scales and 2) following the steps for creating performance scales.

The Prerequisites for Creating Performance Scales

There are three prerequisites for creating performance scales: 1) understanding the structure of a scale, 2) understanding how to use the taxonomy, and 3) using the taxonomy to determine the cognitive complexity of the standard on which you will base your scale.

Understanding the Structure of a Scale

To create your own performance scales, first explore the structure of a scale. A scale has three critical attributes: 1) distinct levels of knowledge and skills relative to achieving the standard, 2) a progression of learning, and 3) generally a focus on one measurement topic.

Recall the three types of targets you created in the previous section. Figure M shows how the target types are incorporated into the designated levels of the scale. The learning goal targets that align with the cognitive level of the standard are placed at level 3.0 on the scale. Then, foundational targets and simpler content are placed at level 2.0. Finally, the cognitively complex targets that require inferences and application that go deeper into the content of the learning goal targets are placed at level 4.0. Figure M can serve as a helpful resource until you have internalized the levels of a performance scale.

Figure M: Performance Scale Showing Targets and Definitions

Level	Type of Target	Description of the Target
4.0	Cognitively Complex Target	Target that reaches above the cognitive level of the standard that involves making in-depth inferences or applications
3.0	Learning Goal Target	Target that aligns with the cognitive level of the standard
2.0	Foundational Target	Target that builds to the standard (critical processes, necessary background information, essential vocabulary) underpinning the learning goal at cognitive levels below the standard
1.0	With help, partial success at level 2.0 content and level 3.0 content	
0.0	Even with help, no success	

Understand the Structure of the New Taxonomy

A taxonomy is an organization or categorization system. In the context of creating performance scales, the taxonomy has categorized four levels of processing within a specific cognitive system known as the New Taxonomy, pictured in Figure N. Note that each level contains several thinking processes. With the exception of the retrieval level, all of the processes are discrete.

Figure N: The New Taxonomy

Knowledge Utilization

Decision Making, Problem Solving, Experimenting, and Investigating

Analysis

Matching, Classifying, Analyzing Errors, Generalizing, and Specifying

Comprehension

Integrating and Symbolizing

Retrieval

Executing, Recalling, and Recognizing

Work your way through the four levels using the following descriptive text to guide you.

Retrieval. The retrieval level of the taxonomy contains three basic types of thinking processes: executing, recalling, and recognizing. These processes are hierarchical in nature. That is, for your students to execute some type of procedural knowledge, they must first be able to recognize and then recall the various aspects of it. As you use the taxonomy to help you identify the cognitive complexity of a specific standard, keep the hierarchy of the retrieval level in mind. At this level of thinking, there is no expectation that students will demonstrate the knowledge in depth or understand the basic structure of the knowledge.

Comprehension. Comprehension is the next level beyond the retrieval level. At the comprehension level, students integrate and symbolize their knowledge. Students are able to identify the critical and essential information as opposed to the noncritical or nonessential information.

Analysis. At the third level of the taxonomy, analysis involves students examining knowledge with the intent of generating new conclusions. This is where reasoned extensions of knowledge occur and can be accomplished through matching, classifying, analyzing errors, and generalizing or specifying activities.

Knowledge Utilization. The highest and most cognitively complex of the four cognitive levels in the taxonomy is knowledge utilization. The thinking processes at this level require that students apply their knowledge in specific situations to include decision making, problem solving, experimenting, or investigating.

Determine the Cognitive Complexity of a Standard Using the Taxonomy

Now that you are beginning to understand the structure of a performance scale as illustrated in Figure M and are mastering the levels of the taxonomy in Figure N, your final task, in anticipation of creating a performance scale, is to gain a basic understanding of how to determine the cognitive complexity of the standard. Take your time with this process and know that if you cannot wrap your brain around it the first time, there will be other opportunities throughout this guide. The cognitive complexity of a standard is derived by identifying the thinking processes inherent in the verbs found in the learning goal targets, and then deciding how a specific thinking process fits into one of the four levels in the taxonomy. After you have identified the taxonomy levels for all of the targets, the one or more targets that match with the highest cognitive level in the taxonomy will automatically become learning goal targets. Although the verbs in the learning goal targets of a standard will almost always lead you straight to the appropriate level of the taxonomy, and thus to the cognitive complexity of the standard, do not overlook the importance of the objects of those verbs. There may be subtle nuances that, if overlooked, can inadvertently lead you to water down and totally change the intent and cognitive level of the standard.

For example, consider the two learning goal targets from the earlier example of the English language arts standards for kindergarten: 1) ask questions about key details in a text and 2) answer questions about key details in a text. At first glance, *answer questions about key details in a text* might seem to be at the Retrieval: recalling level of the taxonomy. However, if you reread the learning goal target more carefully, you will discover that the object of the verb in this target, "questions about key details in a text," indicates a much higher level of cognitive complexity than merely retrieving and recalling. The clue lies in the phrase "key details." Students who are expected to answer questions about key details must understand the difference between important information and trivial details, a process at the higher cognitive level of Comprehension: integrating.

Take a moment to review the three prerequisites for creating a performance scale:

- understand how a performance scale is structured

- understand how the taxonomy works

- understand how to use the taxonomy to determine the cognitive complexity of a standard

Just ahead, you will find the steps for creating a performance scale. You can use the following sections in two ways: 1) to mentally walk through the creation of a performance scale using the explanations and examples or 2) to actually follow the steps using the provided templates to create a performance scale for a standard you have selected.

The Steps for Creating a Performance Scale

In anticipation of walking through the creation of a performance scale using the examples and in-depth explanations of the various steps, assemble the following materials: Figure M, Performance Scale Showing Targets and Definitions, and Figure N, The New Taxonomy.

If you have previously attended trainings on how to create targets and scales or worked with colleagues to create performance scales, you may be ready to use Figure O, Quick Steps for Creating a Performance Scale. However, take time to review the examples and explanations of performance scales that will provide deeper insights into the process. Figure O is somewhat like the one-page set-up instructions you find packaged with many different products for consumers who may already know the basics and want to get started as quickly as possible.

Figure O: Quick Steps for Creating a Performance Scale

Step	Directions
1	Record the learning goal targets you have unpacked from your selected standard(s) on the taxonomy levels template (Figure P).
2	Identify the taxonomy levels of all of the learning goal targets you have created from your selected standard(s) using the New Taxonomy (Figure N) and record them in the second column of the taxonomy levels template (Figure P).
3	Identify the target(s) on the template that are at the highest level in the taxonomy and record a 3.0 in the third column of the taxonomy levels template.
4	Assign and record a 2.0 scale level to the remaining targets on the taxonomy levels template.
5	Enter the complete text of the standard(s) in the top row of the performance scale template (Figure Q).
6	Transfer the 3.0 learning goal targets from the taxonomy levels template to the 3.0 level of performance scale template beneath the phrase *students will be able to*. Boldface the verbs in each of the learning goal targets.
7	Transfer the 2.0 learning goal targets from the taxonomy levels template to the 2.0 level of the performance scale template, recording them under the phrase *students will be able to*.
8	Assemble the previously identified foundational targets that were reconceptualized as foundational knowledge and foundational processes and incorporate them into the 2.0 level of the performance scale template. Record the foundational knowledge under the phrase *students will understand*. Record the foundational processes under the phrase *students will be able to*.
9	Assemble the previously identified cognitively complex targets and record them in the 4.0 level of the performance scale template.

There are two templates that accompany the quick steps in Figure O: a taxonomy levels template (Figure P) and a performance scale template (Figure Q). Figure P is a blank copy of a form that you will eventually complete on your own. It is a prerequisite for creating a performance scale.

Figure P: Taxonomy Levels Template

Learning Goal Target	Taxonomy Level	Scale Level

Figure Q is a blank copy of a performance scale that you will eventually create on your own.

Figure Q: Performance Scale Template

	Standards
4.0	Students will be able to:
3.0	Students will be able to:
2.0	Students will recognize or recall specific vocabulary: Students will be able to:
1.0	With help, partial success at level 2.0 content and level 3.0 content
0.0	Even with help, no success

The quick steps in Figure O tell you everything you need to do to create a performance scale, including how to complete both of the templates (Figures P and Q). However, they will not tell you *why* you are doing it. Look them over for the big picture, but then take time to conceptualize the process using the following four steps.

There are four conceptual steps to creating a performance scale: 1) identify the taxonomy levels of the targets, 2) determine the scale levels of the targets, 3) integrate the previously identified foundational targets, and 4) insert previously identified cognitively complex targets.

Step 1: Identify the Taxonomy Levels of the Targets

The first step to creating a performance scale is identifying the taxonomy levels of all learning goal targets that have been created from a standard. This involves analyzing the actions required to reach proficiency specified in the standard.

Figure R provides an example of the identified taxonomy levels of the elementary English language arts literacy goal target exemplified earlier in the guide. Notice that the verbs in the learning goal targets are in bold print. They contain the information needed to identify the taxonomy levels.

Figure R: Taxonomy Levels of Learning Goal Targets for Kindergarten English Language Arts

Learning Goal Target Elementary – English Language Arts	Taxonomy Level	Scale Level
Identify characters in a story	Retrieval: recognizing	2.0
Identify settings in a story	Retrieval: recognizing	2.0
Identify major events in a story	Retrieval: recognizing	2.0
Ask questions about key details in a text	Comprehension: integrating	3.0
Answer questions about key details in a text	Comprehension: integrating	3.0

Compare the verbs in the learning goal targets with the four levels of the taxonomy, and determine which taxonomy level best matches the verb. For example, in Figure R the verb *identify* found in three of the learning goal targets correlates with the bottom thinking step of the retrieval level in the taxonomy: Retrieval: recognizing. This taxonomy level is recorded in the first three rows of Figure R. The verbs *ask* and *answer* in Figure R correlate with the Comprehension: integrating level of the taxonomy.

Step 2: Determine the Scale Levels of the Learning Goal Targets

The second step in creating a performance scale is to determine the scale levels of the various learning goal targets. This can be accomplished by identifying the learning goal target(s) that correlate with the highest taxonomy level. Figure S provides an example of how this can be done.

Figure S: Taxonomy Levels of Middle School Mathematics Learning Goal Targets

Learning Goal Target Middle School – Mathematics	Taxonomy Level	Scale Level
Know numbers that are not rational are called *irrational*	Retrieval: recalling	2.0
Understand informally that every number has a decimal expansion	Comprehension: integrating	2.0
Show that the decimal expansion repeats eventually for rational numbers	Retrieval: executing	2.0
Convert a decimal expansion, which repeats eventually into a rational number	Retrieval: executing	2.0
Compare the size of irrational numbers using rational approximations	Analysis: matching	3.0
Locate irrational numbers approximately on a number line diagram	Retrieval: executing	2.0
Estimate the value of irrational expressions (e.g., π^2)	Analysis: specifying	3.0

Note that in Figure S, there are two learning goal targets at the analysis level—Analysis:matching and Analysis: specifying—while the remaining targets correlate with lower cognitive levels: Retrieval: recall, Retrieval: executing, and Comprehension: integrating.

The guiding principle that dictates how you assign a scale level to a learning goal target is this: The learning goal targets at the highest cognitive level in the taxonomy are automatically placed at level 3.0 of the performance scale.

In Figure S, the cognitive level of the standard correlates with the analysis level of the taxonomy: Analysis: matching and Analysis: specifying.

Figure T provides an example showing a standard where the majority of the created learning goal targets will be placed at level 3.0 of the standard. As you might have predicted, the learning goal targets at the cognitive level of the standard are more numerous. Four of the five learning goal targets correlate with the Analysis: matching level of the taxonomy. If you need clarification, refer to the New Taxonomy in Figure N (page 27) to review how the cognitive levels of the learning goal targets were identified.

Figure T: Taxonomy Levels of High School Biology Learning Goal Targets

Learning Goal Target High School – Biology	Taxonomy Level	Scale Level
Relate structure to function for the components of plant and animal cells	Analysis: matching	3.0
Explain the role of cell membranes as a highly selective barrier	Comprehension: integrating	2.0
Compare and **contrast** the general structures of plant and animal cells	Analysis: matching	3.0
Compare and **contrast** the general structures of prokaryotic and eukaryotic cells	Analysis: matching	3.0
Compare and **contrast** structure and function of various types of microscopes	Analysis: matching	3.0

Step 3: Integrate the Previously Identified Foundational Targets

The integration of the foundational targets that were previously identified during the creation of learning targets takes place in step 3. The vocabulary and basic processes determined when creating the foundational targets should be incorporated into level 2.0 of the performance scale along with the identified learning goal targets from the previous step that correlate with lower cognitive processing levels in the taxonomy.

Figure U illustrates the foundational knowledge and processes that have been incorporated into the completed performance scale for high school biology, found in Figure V.

Figure U: Foundational Targets for High School Biology

High School – Biology	Grades: Ninth–Twelfth

(CPALMS: Life Science SC.912.L.14.2): Relate structure to function for the components of plant and animal cells. **Explain** the role of cell membranes as a highly selective barrier (passive and active transport).

(CPALMS: Life Science SC.912.L.14.3): Compare and **contrast** the general structures of plant and animal cells. **Compare** and **contrast** the general structures of prokaryotic and eukaryotic cells.

(CPALMS: Life Science SC.912.L.14.4): Compare and **contrast** structure and function of various types of microscopes.

Foundational Knowledge Students will understand:	Foundational Processes Students will be able to:
• Vocabulary: *plant cells, animal cells, eukaryotic cells, cell membrane (plasma membrane), highly selective barrier, permeable, active transport, passive transport, cell wall, cytoplasm, ribosomes, nucleus, nuclear membrane, nucleolus, chromatic, endoplasmic reticulum, microtubules, microfilaments, vacuoles, mitochondria, Golgi apparatus, chloroplasts, lysosomes, hypotonic, hypertonic, isotonic solutions, component, organelle, chromosomes, phospholipid, polar, molecule, vesicles* • Components of a eukaryotic cell • Structures and functions of the components of plant and animal cells • Cell membrane is a highly selective barrier • Materials pass in and out of a cell	• **Relate** structure to function for the components of plant and animal cells • **Explain** the role of cell membranes as a highly selective barrier (passive and active transport) • **Compare** and **contrast** the general structures of plant and animal cells • **Compare** and **contrast** the general structures of prokaryotic and eukaryotic cells • **Compare** and **contrast** structure and function of various types of microscopes

Figure V displays a completed performance scale for high school biology standards. Notice that the foundational knowledge in Figure U has been placed in level 2.0. This knowledge consists of terms and concepts that students will need to understand either by recognizing or by recalling them during their reading, labs, and lessons. Note that the four bullet points following the foundational vocabulary have been reworded to become processes that students will be able to do at the foundational level to include identifying and describing various concepts. Recall that the foundational processes in Figure U at the cognitive level of the standard have been reframed as the 3.0 learning goal targets in level 3.0 of the performance scale.

Figure V: Performance Scale for High School Biology Standards

4.0	Students will be able to: **Research** ways that cell components are used in medical advancement.
3.0	Students will be able to: ● **Compare** and **contrast** the general structures of plant and animal cells. **(SC.912.L.14.3)** ● **Generalize** the relationship between the structure and function of the components of plant and animal cells. **(SC.912.L.14.2)** ● **Compare** and **contrast** the structures found in prokaryotic cells and eukaryotic cells. **(SC.912.L.14.3)** ● **Differentiate** between active and passive transport. **(SC.912.L.14.2)** ● **Create** an analogy for the cell membranes as role as a barrier. **(SC.912.L.14.2)** ● **Compare** and **construct** structure and function of various types of microscopes. **(SC.912.L.14.4)**
2.0	Students will **recognize** or **recall** specific vocabulary, including: ● *plant cells, animal cells, eukaryotic cells, cell membrane (plasma membrane), highly selective barrier, permeable, active transport, passive transport, cell wall, cytoplasm, ribosomes, nucleus, nuclear membrane, nucleolus, chromatic, endoplasmic reticulum, microtubules, microfilaments, vacuoles, mitochondria, Golgi apparatus, chloroplasts, lysosomes, hypotonic, hypertonic, isotonic solutions, component, organelle, chromosomes, phospholipid, polar, molecule, vesicles* In addition, students will **recognize** or **recall** specific affixes: ● *cyto-, nuc-, chroma-, micro-, mito-, vac-, chloro-, lyso-, hypo-, hyper-, iso-, pro-, eu-, trans-* Students will be able to: ● **Identify** the components of a eukaryotic cell (cell wall, cytoplasm, ribosomes, nucleus, nuclear envelope, nucleolus, chromatic, endoplasmic reticulum, microtubules, microfilaments, vacuoles, mitochondria, Golgi apparatus, chloroplasts, lysosomes). **(SC.912.L.14.3)** ● **Describe** the relationship between the structures and functions of the components of plant and animal cells. **(SC.912.L.14.2)** ● **Describe** how the cell membrane is a highly selective barrier. **(SC.912.L.14.2)** ● **Identify** how materials pass in and out of a cell (passive and active transport). **(SC.912.L.14.2)**
1.0	With help, partial success at level 2.0 content and level 3.0 content
0.0	Even with help, no success

Take care at this point during the creation of a performance scale to ensure that the levels of processing of the targets as they move through the foundational targets to the learning goal targets reflect a clear and comprehensive progression in thinking processes. There should be no gaps between the levels of processing that the targets require. Use the following guidelines to prevent gaps from occurring:

- If the learning goal targets are determined to be at the analysis level or higher on the taxonomy, the foundational targets must include both the retrieval and comprehension levels of processing. See an example of this by comparing the Taxonomy Levels of Middle School Mathematics learning goal targets in Figure S (page 33) and its corresponding performance scale in Figure W.

Figure W: Performance Scale for Middle School Mathematics Learning Goal Targets

Middle School – Mathematics	Grade: Eighth

(CCSS.Math.8.NS.A.1): Know that numbers that are not rational are called irrational. Understand informally that every number has a decimal expansion; for rational numbers show that the decimal expansion repeats eventually, and convert a decimal expansion which repeats eventually into a rational number.

(CCSS.Math.8.NS.A.2): Use rational approximations of irrational numbers to compare the size of irrational numbers, locate them approximately on a number line diagram, and estimate the value of expressions (e.g., π^2).

4.0	Students will be able to: • *Investigate* the outcome of applying properties (addition, subtraction, multiplication, division) to both rational and irrational numbers
3.0	Students will be able to: • *Compare* the size of irrational numbers using rational approximations • *Estimate* the value of irrational expressions (e.g.,)
2.0	Students will *recognize* or *recall* specific vocabulary, including: • *rational numbers, irrational numbers, decimal expansion, convert, nonrepeating decimal, nonterminating decimal* Students will be able to: • *Understand* informally that every number has decimal expansion • *Locate* irrational numbers approximately on a number line diagram • *Convert* a decimal expansion which repeats eventually into a rational number • *Show* that decimal expansion repeats eventually for rational numbers • *Know* that numbers that are not rational are called irrational
1.0	With help, partial success at level 2.0 content and level 3.0 content
0.0	Even with help, no success

- If the learning goal target is determined to be at the integrating level of comprehension, the foundational targets must include the knowledge and skills at the retrieval level of the taxonomy. See an example of this by comparing Figure R, Taxonomy Levels of Learning Goal Targets for Kindergarten English Language Arts, and its corresponding performance scale in Figure X.

Figure X: Performance Scale for Kindergarten English Language Arts Standards

Elementary – English Language Arts	Grade: Kindergarten

(CCSS.ELA-Literacy.RL.K.3): With prompting and support, identify characters, settings and major events in a story.

(CCSS.ELA-Literacy RL.K.1): With prompting and support, ask and answer questions about key details in a text.

4.0	With prompting and support students will be able to: • ***Compare and contrast*** key details of a story, including characters, settings, and major events

3.0	With prompting and support students will be able to:
	• ***Ask and answer*** questions about key details in a text about:
	   – characters in a story
	   – settings in a story
	   – major events in a story

2.0	Students will ***recognize*** or ***recall*** specific vocabulary, including:
	• *story, setting, characters, events, ask, answer, detail, question, text*
	
	With prompting and support, students will be able to:
	• Answer teacher-provided questions about key details in text
	   – ***Identify*** characters in a story
	   – ***Identify*** settings in a story
	   – ***Identify*** major events in a story

1.0	With help, partial success at level 2.0 content and level 3.0 content
0.0	Even with help, no success

Step 4: Insert the Previously Identified Cognitively Complex Targets

The final step in creating the performance scale is to place the more rigorous targets at the highest level of the scale. These targets extend the level of learning progression beyond the learning goal targets, requiring students to apply and integrate the content of the standard. Review the three performance scales shown previously and note how the level 4.0 targets vary according to the cognitive complexity of the standard. At the kindergarten level, the English language arts level 4.0 target is compare and contrast key details of a story, including characters, settings, and major events. The cognitive complexity of the targets in level 3.0 provides the standard's expectations, and level 4.0 must build on level 3.0.

The level 4.0 target for the middle school math performance scale is investigate the outcome of applying properties (addition, subtraction, multiplication, division) to both rational and irrational numbers. The cognitive complexity of the targets at level 3.0 correlate with the analysis level of the taxonomy. That automatically dictates developing a level 4.0 target at the knowledge utilization level and, in the case of this cognitively complex target, Knowledge utilization: investigating.

The level 4.0 target for the high school biology performance scale is research ways that cell components are used in medical advancement. The cognitive complexity of the targets at level 3.0 of the biology standards correlates with the analysis level of the taxonomy. As in the middle school scale, a 3.0 cognitive complexity of analysis dictates creating a cognitively complex target at Knowledge utilization: investigating.

To recap, the performance scale creation process essentially consists of identifying the taxonomy level of the standard and the teacher-created learning goal targets and sequencing those targets to create a continuum of learning that progresses in cognition.

Level 3.0 on the scale contains the skills needed to demonstrate the cognitive complexity of the standard. Level 2.0 contains the knowledge and basic processes that lay the learning foundation that builds to the standard and is therefore composed of the cognitive processes below those at level 3.0 on the scale. Level 4.0 on the scale includes knowledge and skills that will either deepen the thinking of the standard or, in the case of more complex content, change the context in which the standard will be applied.

PART II

USING LEARNING TARGETS AND PERFORMANCE SCALES

If you have skipped from the beginning of this guide to Part II because you are eager to find ways to implement learning targets and performance scales in your classroom, you will not be disappointed. Hopefully, you have gained a solid understanding about how to create targets and scales. Effective implementation rests on the care you have taken to understand how to create effective targets and scales based on selected standards.

There are many ways to help your students understand and use learning targets and performance scales to become more self-managed and independent in their learning. The approaches you choose to use to explain targets and scales and then make them an integral part of your instructional toolbox will vary and advance as you learn to implement this strategy in your classroom. These various ways or options are called instructional techniques:

- Instructional Technique 1: Routines for Using Targets and Scales

- Instructional Technique 2: Using Teacher-Created Targets and Scales

- Instructional Technique 3: Using Student-Friendly Scales

- Instructional Technique 4: Using Student-Generated Scales

All of the above techniques are similarly organized and include the following components:

- a brief introduction to the technique

- ways to effectively create the technique

- common mistakes to avoid as you implement the technique

- examples and nonexamples from elementary and secondary classrooms using selected learning targets or performance scales based on various standards

- ways to monitor for the desired result

- a scale for monitoring students

- ways to scaffold and extend instruction to meet the needs of students

ROUTINES FOR USING TARGETS AND SCALES

The effective implementation of a performance scale and the set of learning targets on which it is based requires that you know precisely how to communicate the purpose and value of these tools to your students in clear and understandable ways. The most efficient way to communicate the various aspects of a scale and its targets to your students is through using a variety of routines. A routine in the context of this guide is a procedure used by teachers during instruction to precisely communicate the what, why, and how of a specific aspect of understanding and using a scale and its targets. Helping students understand what the routine is, why it is being implemented, and how it will be used is imperative to using targets and scales in your classroom.

How to Effectively Use Classroom Routines for Implementing Targets and Scales

There are five different routines that can help you and your students realize the power of a scale and its targets to ensure student mastery of critical content.

1. Explain the What, Why, and How of a Scale and Its Targets

WHAT: A scale and its targets are tools that communicate learning expectations and detail the progression of learning to follow to reach success with the content.

WHY: A scale and its targets provide focused direction and structure that makes learning more visible to everyone. These tools help students self-regulate their learning and motivate a growth mindset that will eventually empower them to take control of their own learning.

HOW: Following are some helpful hints showing how to explain the what, how, and why of a scale and its targets to your students:

- Spend time developing the explanation you give your students during your initial implementation.

- Choose your terms carefully and be consistent in the way you use them.

- Select a simile, if appropriate: A scale is like a road map, a scale is like our "to do" list, or a scale is like a yardstick on which we measure our learning.

- Keep your introduction simple. Not every student will understand every nuance of a scale and its targets on the first day, and you will often repeat these words. Memorize this routine so it becomes second nature to you.

2. Make the Scale and Its Learning Targets Accessible to Students

WHAT: Accessibility means doing two things: 1) having physical copies and artifacts that explain and relate to the goal within easy reach of you and your students and 2) making the language and structure of the scale and targets as accessible as you can to students through creating student-friendly scales that use simpler terms or pictures to convey the intent of a standard. A copy of the learning goals and scale needs to be within arm's reach at all times during instruction. Both you and your students should be able to view the tool as often as needed. The targets on the scale should be clearly and concisely written to avoid confusion or misdirection when referenced.

WHY: Accessibility to the performance scale is imperative if using it is to become a natural practice. If you and your students are constantly reminded of the scale, it will become a well-used document. Accessibility will lead to familiarity, and familiarity will lead to regular usage. Students will learn to rely on the structure the tool provides and refer to the targets and scale whenever they need direction or clarification.

HOW: Following are some helpful hints showing how to make a scale and its targets accessible in your classroom:

- Post a copy of the current scale and its targets somewhere for easy reference.

- Create a copy for your whiteboard so you can readily point to it during instruction.

- If academic language is too difficult, create a student-friendly scale that is more understandable and/or add graphics to scaffold students' understanding of the targets.

- Add the applicable learning target to classroom activity and assignment sheets to make it more accessible to both you and your students.

- Prepare handouts for students and their parents (if appropriate) containing the scale and its targets. Ask students to keep a copy in their academic notebooks.

3. Begin and Close Each Lesson With a Focus on the Target

WHAT: To clearly communicate and emphasize the purpose of daily instruction, begin each lesson with a brief explanation connecting that day's lesson to a target on the scale. Then, when you are winding up the lesson, remind students of the target and together "put it back on the scale."

WHY: Making a connection between the content to be covered that day and the learning targets embedded in the scale provides both direction and background for students. Students will not have to wonder "why they need to know this" or "when they would ever use this" if the teacher makes a connection between the learning goal and the lesson.

HOW: Following are some helpful hints showing how to begin each lesson with a target focus:

- Provide an overview of the day's lesson, and then ask students to tell their partners what the target for the lesson will be.

- Provide a statement informing students of the focus of the lesson.

- Build in a reference to the previous day's learning target and then segue to the day's target: *Yesterday we worked on (yesterday's target). Today we will continue our study by focusing on (today's target).*

- Communicate the target and give students a preview of your expectations for them during the lesson: *Our lesson today focuses on (today's target). At the end of the lesson, I will ask you to identify the connections you made to (today's target), so let's get focused!*

- Close each lesson by going back to the performance scale and fitting the lesson's target into the context of the learning progression of the scale.

4. Relate Instruction to the Target

WHAT: Purposeful reminders relating the instruction, activities, and assignments to the learning targets are needed to integrate this routine into the culture of your classroom. Simply announcing the target focus at the beginning of the lesson is not enough. Correlation to the learning target should be made whenever the opportunity arises.

WHY: Relating the direct instruction and all other tasks students are completing helps to accentuate the connection between classroom activities and the learning target. Understanding the purpose behind activities often motivates and empowers students to identify with and personalize their learning. This continuous refocusing not only reengages students, but also helps them integrate the learning process and self-regulate their behavior.

HOW: Following are some helpful hints showing how to consistently use the routine of relating instruction to the target:

- Intentionally plan to include purposeful reminders by adding sticky notes in your plan book or setting a timer to remind yourself to relate your instruction to the target.

- Quietly ask a reliable student to periodically raise his hand to ask the question: *Mrs. B, how is what you are talking about right now related to the learning target you identified at the beginning of class?*

- Use quick writes, small group discussions, or some other activity to quickly refocus learning on the target and forge a relationship between the activity and the target.

- Challenge students at the beginning of the class period to write down any connections between the lesson and the learning target. Give extra credit points for students who are able to discover a connection.

5. Refer to the Learning Progression of the Scale

WHAT: Consistently build students' awareness of how their learning is building toward an ultimate goal or destination. Reference should be made to the progression of learning embedded in the scale that provides the steps students need to follow to advance their understanding of the content the standard requires.

WHY: Do not teach learning targets in isolation. Students should be made aware of the connections between the learning targets and classroom activities as well as how the connections between targets advance their knowledge of the content. Consistently remind students of the big picture and explain as often as needed that they must master each target at level 2.0 to reach the learning goal target of the standard at level 3.0. Your skillful references to a scale's learning progression will motivate and instill a growth mindset in your students.

HOW: Following are some helpful hints showing how to consistently use the routine of referring to the progression of learning in a scale:

- Ask students how the activity they are doing relates to what they learned previously or to the learning targets yet to come.

- Encourage and expect students to take ownership of their learning by relating the knowledge they have gained to the learning progression of the scale to determine areas of weakness or possible misconceptions that might interfere with their successful mastery of the learning goal target.

- Ask students to summarize what they have learned over a period of time, relating it to the learning progression evident in the scale.

- Plan a specific activity related to the learning progression in the scale such as using the performance scale to review for a test.

- Project a template of a performance scale on a magnetic whiteboard on which the scale is always present during instruction. Create magnetic targets that can be affixed to the board.

- Physically remove the target being taught in a day's lesson and display it to students. Keep the target handy to remind students of the lesson's focus.

- At the close of the lesson, pick up the target and place it on the scale at its appropriate level.

Common Mistakes

Using classroom routines during your implementation of a scale and its targets requires thoughtful planning to ensure that the ways in which you communicate the purpose and use of these tools produces the most beneficial results with your students. The most common mistakes to avoid when creating this routine are:

- When first introducing the learning targets and scale to students, the teacher does not explain the purpose or the *what*, *why*, and *how* of a routine.

- The teacher fails to purposely model how to use the learning targets and performance scale as an instructional resource tool to provide structure to the learning environment.

- The teacher spends an excessive amount of time or overwhelms students with too much information instead of providing a brief overview or reference to the tool.

- The teacher does not make a conscious effort to relate instruction to the focus targets or learning goal targets or make reference to the learning progression in the scale.

- The teacher does not make the learning goals or performance scale assessable for all students.

Examples and Nonexamples of Using Classroom Routines for Implementing Targets and Scales

The following examples and nonexamples demonstrate ways to integrate learning targets and scales into your classroom community through the use of classroom routines. As you read, consider how the example teachers are effectively using routines and how their nonexample colleagues are making serious mistakes.

Elementary Example of Using Classroom Routines for Implementing Targets and Scales

The academic standard that is the focus in the example classroom is *use information gained from illustrations (e.g., maps, photographs) and the words in a text to demonstrate understanding of the text* (CCSS.ELA-Literacy.RI.3.7). The teacher in this third-grade classroom has been focused on the learning targets of the standard, shown in Figure 1.1.

Figure 1.1: Elementary Example of a Performance Scale for Text Structure and Features

Elementary – English Language Arts	Grade: Third

(CCSS.ELA-Literacy.RI.3.7): *Use* information gained from illustrations (e.g., maps, photographs) and the words in a text to *demonstrate* understanding of the text (e.g., where, when, why, and how key events occur).

4.0	Students will be able to: ● *Invent* an appropriate text feature that corresponds with a selected text and explain how it contributes to an understanding of the text

3.0	Students will be able to:
	● Make inferences to *demonstrate* understanding of the text by:
	  – *Using* information gained from illustrations
	  – *Using* information gained from words in a text

2.0	Students will *recognize* or *recall* specific vocabulary, including: ● *information, map, photograph, chart, graph, image, pamphlet, timeline* Students will perform basic processes such as: ● *Identify* specific text features ● *Describe* the purpose of text features ● *Explain* how specific images clarify a text ● *Explain* how specific images contribute to a text
1.0	With help, partial success at level 2.0 content and level 3.0 content
0.0	Even with help, no success

She has projected this scale on her whiteboard. Today, she is focused on leading students to make connections between the various assignments and tasks they have been working on during the past week and the learning targets and their placement on the scale. She has prepared laminated task cards and identified the appropriate learning target and its level at the top of each card. Here is how she introduces her lesson:

> Class, we've been working on a lot of different activities related to text features. I have a stack of task/assignment cards that you will recognize as I hold them up. Throughout this past week, you have completed these tasks and assignments. Each of these assignments was related to a certain level on our scale. Some tasks were level 2.0 tasks, some were level 3.0, and there were also some that were level 4.0.
>
> I'm going to hold up a card right next to that learning target. Then I'm going to count to three, and I want you to show me with your fingers the level of this assignment. You can hold up two, three, or even four fingers depending on the cognitive level of the task.

The teacher holds up an activity card that corresponds to a level 3.0 target: using information gained from illustrations. Most of the students are able to identify it as a level 3.0 activity. She then shows students a level 2.0 activity and once again asks them to hold up the number of fingers that correspond to the scale level of the task. She goes on to ask students:

> What is the difference between a level 2.0 and a level 3.0 activity? Talk with your partner about that difference. As I was walking around and listening to your conversations, I heard Emily tell her partner the difference between level 2.0 and level 3.0 activities. Emily, would you share that with the class, please?

Emily answers, "Level 2.0 is kind of the plan for where we were going, and we just had to learn about things we didn't know. In level 3.0, we had to use what we learned and do things with the learning." The teacher continues:

> Good thinking. Today we're going to go deeper into working with text features, and we're going to invent a text feature that goes along with some text. We'll be working at level 4.0 and using all of the knowledge and skills we've learned from levels 2.0 and 3.0. I haven't revealed that text to you yet, but I soon will.

The teacher has assembled samples of a multitude of text features across the front of the room that will undoubtedly scaffold her students' ability to complete this more cognitively complex task.

Elementary Nonexample of Using Routines for Implementing Targets and Scales

The nonexample third-grade teacher is working with the same standard and performance scale in the example classroom. He has assembled a variety of examples of these features, and students have completed an equal number of activities related to the learning targets as the students in the example class. The teacher begins his lesson this way:

> Good morning, class. Today we're going to invent a text feature. I'm going to give you some text to read, and then you will invent the text feature and explain how it will help readers who would use your invented text feature to understand the text. Please get into your work groups and get started.

The nonexample teacher assumes a great deal of knowledge and understanding on the part of his students that may or may not be present. However, without probing his students' thinking to see if they are making connections between classroom activities and the scale and understanding the progression of learning within the scale, the purpose of the activity may well be left unfulfilled.

Secondary Example of Using Routines for Implementing Targets and Scales

The academic standard that is the focus of this secondary example is displayed at the top of the teacher-created performance scale in Figure 1.2. Students have received copies of the scale and stapled them into their academic notebooks. The teacher has also created a poster-sized version that is permanently displayed on a bulletin board. In addition, she projects the scale on her whiteboard so she can situate the target for today's lesson in the broader context of the standard and the performance scale. She consistently uses the same routines as she integrates the usage of a scale and its targets into her instruction.

Figure 1.2: Secondary Example of a Performance Scale for Reading/Comprehension of Text

(TEKS ELAR 6.11): Reading/Comprehension of Informational Text/Persuasive Text Students analyze, make inferences and draw conclusions about persuasive text and provide evidence from text to support their analysis. Students are expected to: (A) compare and contrast the structure and viewpoints of two different authors writing for the same purpose, noting the stated claim and supporting evidence; and (B) identify simple faulty reasoning used in persuasive texts.	
4.0	Students will be able to: ● **Make** and **defend** a decision about which of two persuasive texts written for the same purpose by different authors provides the best or most beneficial information

3.0	Students will be able to:
	● **Analyze, make inferences,** and **draw conclusions** about persuasive text and provide evidence from the text to support their analysis as they:
	  – **Compare** and **contrast** the structure used by two authors writing for the same purpose, noting the stated claim and supporting evidence
	  – **Compare** and **contrast** the viewpoints of two authors writing for the same purpose, noting the stated claim and supporting evidence

2.0	Students will **recognize** or **recall** specific vocabulary, including: ● *faulty reasoning, overgeneralization, illogical conclusion, personal bias, author's purpose, stated purpose, implied purpose, viewpoint, persuasive technique* Students will be able to: ● **Use** reading strategies to support interpretation of texts ● **Identify** a stated claim ● **Identify** simple faulty reasoning used in persuasive texts ● **Identify** the structure of a text (sequence, compare and contrast, cause and effect, problem and solution, and description) ● **Describe** how authors use structure and viewpoint to influence attitudes, emotions, or actions of a specific audience ● **Explain** the effectiveness of the persuasive techniques based on audience, purpose, and message
1.0	With help, partial success at level 2.0 content and level 3.0 content
0.0	Even with help, no success

The specific learning target for the current lesson is on level 2.0: *identify simple faulty reasoning used in persuasive texts.*

The students were previously introduced to the scale and have been working on the foundational target: *use reading strategies to support interpretation of texts.*

> Class, you just worked with a partner to read short text excerpts in which I asked you to look for various types of faulty reasoning we've learned about. I want you to turn and talk to your partner and discuss the following question: What did this activity help you learn?

The teacher walks around the room and listens to partner conversations to determine whether students are able to connect the recent activity to the appropriate target on the scale. When the partner conversations begin to lull, the teacher randomly calls on students to share their responses to the whole group to verify the correct target and level of the scale. She continues this way:

> Nice job. Now I want you to think about what is required at the next level of the scale—3.0. What do you need to learn next to reach that goal? In a quick write, I want you to tell me how today's activity relates to the learning target and what else you need to learn to reach the next target. I'll write the sentence starters we've used before on the board to help you focus.

The teacher writes the following statements on the board: Today's activity relates to _____ because I learned _____. To move forward in my learning, I now need to _____.

The teacher collects and reads the quick write summaries to determine whether the students can explain how the activity relates to its aligned learning target and whether they understand what they need to learn next to advance toward the learning goal target. The sentence starters provide evidence of whether students are using the targets and scales to integrate the learning process and self-regulate their learning of persuasive texts.

Secondary Nonexample of Developing Routines for Using Targets and Scales

The teacher in this nonexample is using the same scale to plan her lessons and has also posted a copy on the wall for easy viewing. She rarely makes reference to the learning targets or scale, but wants to make it accessible in case it is needed. The students have completed the same activities throughout the unit as the students from the example classroom.

> Class, you just worked with a partner to read short text excerpts in which I asked you to look for the various types of faulty reasoning we've learned. In your notebook, I want you to identify which target this activity relates to and explain why you think that. Feel free to use the scale that is posted in the room and look back in your notebooks for help. Spend about five minutes working on your response, and when you are finished, please move to the second activity listed on the board.

The teacher provides no modeling or opportunity for students to share and justify their thinking before beginning the task. There is no evidence that specific routines for using targets and scales has been established, so many students do not understand how to use the tool. The students are left to work independently without guidance or support. If they have never used the scale before for this purpose, they may not be able to connect the activity to the aligned target. If the scale has simply been posted and no discussion or reference to the targets has occurred in previous lessons, the students are no doubt feeling frustrated or anxious. Their artifacts or charts will likely demonstrate an inaccurate understanding of and connection to the targets, indicating a lack of integration and self-regulation skills due to the lack of an established routine.

Determining If Students Understand How to Use Targets and Scales

Well-established routines affix the use of learning targets and performance scales into daily instruction. An effective routine results in students taking ownership of their learning by using targets and scales to make connections and guide their learning process in a self-sufficient manner. Monitoring to determine if the routines developed for using targets and scales in the classroom help students understand the learning goal and what the scale means requires that students demonstrate the connection between the learning targets, activities, and the progression of learning when asked. Here are some student behaviors to monitor to determine whether routines for using targets and scales provide focused direction and structure to the learning environment:

- Without prompting, students make reference to the learning targets to answer questions the teacher poses regarding a lesson or activity.

- Without prompting, students make reference to the scale and the progression of learning between the targets to demonstrate how instruction and learning build toward the learning goal target.

- Students can orally explain or describe in writing the target focus for a lesson.

- Student products demonstrate connections are being made to the learning targets and the progression of learning evident in the scale.

- Students integrate personal use of the tool to independently advance their learning.

Table 1.1 contains a proficiency scale to help you determine the impact on students of developing routines for using targets and scales. Use the scale to refine your practice as you monitor the influence of routines for using targets and scales in your classroom.

Table 1.1: Student Proficiency Scale for Understanding Routines for Using Targets and Scales

Emerging	Fundamental	Desired Result
Students provide responses regarding learning target connections to instruction or an activity.	Students make reference to the learning targets to determine their connections to instruction or an activity.	Students make reference to the learning targets to determine their connection to instruction or an activity and use the tool to self-regulate their learning.
Students intermittently use the tool as a resource to support daily learning.	Students consistently use the tool as a resource to focus and support daily learning.	Students use the tool as a resource to focus and support daily learning and self-regulate their learning.
Students recognize that instruction relates to the learning progression embedded in the scale.	Students can explain how instruction relates to the learning progression embedded in the scale.	Students can explain how instruction and their personal learning experiences relate to the learning progression embedded in the scale to self-regulate their learning.

Scaffold and Extend Instruction to Meet Students' Needs

There may be students who do not understand the routines developed for using targets and scales in the classroom or how to use the tool to self-regulate their learning. In addition, there may be students who innately seem to understand and use the tool with ease. Meeting the needs of these two diverse groups of students requires you to adapt the instruction associated with the routine. Here are some suggestions for providing support or extension to those students.

Scaffolding

- Make small, student-friendly copies of the focus targets and tape them to desks for student reference.

- Ask for student volunteers to model the routine or how they use the tool to self-regulate their learning.

- Provide sentence starters to those who need help relating the activity to the target or the progression of the scale.

Extending

- Ask students to develop a simple routine that uses the tool to provide support or direction when needed to verify connections between targets, activities, and the progression of learning.

- Ask students to create a method of incorporating targets and scales to self-regulate learning that other students could use.

Instructional Technique 2

USING TEACHER-CREATED TARGETS AND SCALES

To this point, you have learned how to create learning targets and performance scales in Part I and acquired various classroom routines in Instructional Technique 1 to jump-start your implementation of targets and scales. This second technique, using the learning targets and performance scales you have created, will help you put together the various routines into a seamless whole to create the big picture. You can view any performance scale you create, whether a simple student-friendly scale showing the progression of learning in a kindergarten English language arts unit, as illustrated earlier in Part I (see Figure X, page 39), or a complex teacher-created scale for a high school biology unit, as shown in an upcoming example in this technique (Figure 2.3).

Some teachers think of a performance scale as a frequently consulted road map leading them and their students on a journey that culminates in the attainment of a challenging academic standard. Other teachers think of scales as living classroom documents that are continually being used and adapted, such as when a teacher discovers the need to add additional targets or subtargets to further support learning one of the targets on the scale. Still others view scales as a daily organizer that provides a framework and structure on which to keep teachers and their students constantly focused as learning is progressing. All of these metaphors incorporate the essence of targets and scales: the identification of what students need to know and be able to do to attain the standard organized into a clear progression of learning targets. Whatever your preferred metaphor, make sure that you remain focused on the learning goal targets with consistency and intensity.

How to Effectively Implement Learning Targets and Performance Scales

The effective implementation of learning targets and performance scales assumes that you are becoming increasingly skilled at creating targets and scales that are consistent with the needs of your students and the cognitive complexity of specific standards. You will be unable to effectively implement this technique if the scales you create are not rigorous and faithful to the intent of the standard. The implementation of targets and scales demands that you engage in the following key teacher behaviors: 1) introduce and explain the scale and its targets to students, 2) help students become familiar with the scale, 3) refer constantly and seamlessly to the targets and scale throughout the lesson, and 4) relate activities and assignments to the targets and scale throughout the lesson.

Introduce and Explain the Scale and Its Targets to Students

Now that you have created the targets and organized the progression of learning embedded in the performance scale, consider how you will introduce and explain the scale and its targets to your unique group of students. This aspect of implementation is paramount to the success of the instructional strategy as a whole.

During the first-time introduction of a scale and its targets to your students, explain the purpose of a scale and its targets. Review the various routines introduced in Instructional Technique 1 and select only one of them to implement. If you have chosen a metaphor to frame your discussion, keep it very simple. A metaphor that resonates for you may be totally incomprehensible to your students.

When introducing and explaining targets and scales to students, do not lose your way by suddenly shifting your emphasis to the specifics of content. Your aim in this step is to introduce and explain the scale and its targets in a general way. There will be time for teaching content once students have grasped two big ideas: 1) Targets are what they need to learn or do by the end of a lesson or unit, and 2) scales show the progression that their learning will follow. The initial introduction of a scale and its targets should move quickly. Reveal and briefly explain the scale and its targets so that every student understands the meaning and expectations within the learning targets.

Eventually students will come to understand how the foundational targets at level 2.0 are related to the learning goal targets at level 3.0 as well as the cognitively complex targets at level 4.0. However, in the beginning keep your explanations direct and explicit.

Ease Students Gradually Into the Challenge of Using Targets and Scales

When you are energized and motivated about implementing a new technique with students, you can mistakenly attempt to tell them everything they need to know in an information-packed, forty-five–minute introduction, complete with as many bells and whistles as you can provide. However, begin cautiously to ensure that your teacher-created scale or even the student-friendly scale you prepared does not overwhelm your students. Recall your own temporary confusion and frustration when you started learning how to create targets and scales. Your students may experience similar emotions if you try to do too much all at once. The mere sight of a scale containing unfamiliar terminology and multiple targets can easily cause students to shut down on the spot if you do not exercise restraint. As important as your students' knowledge about the learning progression that is embedded in the scale may ultimately be, do not expect them to understand the content until actual content instruction has occurred. Emphasize this point to your students. Remember, your students want to succeed in school, despite some of their behaviors to the contrary, and they will quickly become anxious if the targets, scale, and progression appear unobtainable and overpowering when first introduced.

Refer Continually, Effortlessly, and Seamlessly to Targets and Scales During Instruction

Once you have introduced your teacher-created scale and its targets to your students, and then gradually eased them into the implementation process, be alert for any distractions or urgent priorities that can easily subvert your implementation. Once introduced, using targets and scales must become part of your daily routine.

To effectively implement targets and scales, refer to them continually, effortlessly, and seamlessly throughout every lesson. This aspect of implementation is undeniably difficult. Use one or two of the routines introduced in Instructional Technique 1 to help you maintain your focus. *Continually* means referring to a target or aspect of the scale during every lesson. *Effort-lessly* means that you have internalized the instructional strategy on which this guide is based: *creating and using learning targets and performance scales. Seamlessly* means that your students will become quite accustomed to your references and begin to use the thinking and language of the scale in their own answers and discussions.

Remember, the quality and depth of students' understanding and their ultimate mastery of a standard is largely dependent on your continuous, effortless, and seamless modeling of the relationships of critical content to the learning targets and their progression on a performance scale.

Relate Activities to the Targets and Scale Throughout the Lesson

As a beginning teacher, you may well remember laboring for hours to create materials and activities that you eventually discovered contributed nothing at all to your students' attainment of a standard. The first secret to an effective implementation of targets and scales is to ensure that each activity and task a student participates in during a lesson is purposeful and aligned to a specific target on the scale. The second secret to success is helping students understand the purpose and alignment of the targets on the scale. Students who have become accustomed to haphazard and disconnected activities in their classrooms frequently become excited and empowered to take control of their own learning once their teachers reveal to them how everything is connected and gradually builds to the ultimate goal.

Common Mistakes

Here are a few common mistakes teachers make as they implement the learning goals and scales they create in their classroom:

- The teacher simply posts or distributes copies of targets and scales without adequate explanation.

- The teacher confuses introducing the scale with teaching the content.

- The teacher spends an excessive amount of time teaching the scale instead of introducing or briefly referencing it at the beginning of a lesson.

- The teacher introduces or discusses the learning targets and the learning progression of the scale in a way that creates anxiety for students.

- The teacher does not explain the learning targets and their relationship to the learning progression embedded in the scale in such a way that students understand the targets, goal, and scale.

- The teacher does not refer to the targets and their progression on the scale continually and seamlessly during the lesson.

- The teacher does not relate students' activities and tasks to the targets and scale during the lesson.

- The teacher fails to involve and expect students to demonstrate their understanding of the scale and its targets.

Examples and Nonexamples of Using Learning Targets and Performance Scales

Following are two sets of examples and corresponding nonexamples (one elementary and one secondary) of how targets and scales that you create can be implemented in classrooms. As you are reading the examples, note the common mistakes the nonexample teachers make and consider insights you can carry away from the example teachers to your own implementation.

Elementary Example of Using Learning Targets and Performance Scales

The learning targets in this elementary example have been unpacked from the following kindergarten math standards: 1) count to 100 by ones and tens (CCSS.Math.K.CC.A.1); 2) count forward beginning from a given number within the known sequence, instead of having it begin at 1 (CCSS.Math.K.CC.A.2); and 3) write numbers from 0 to 20; represent a number of objects with a written numeral 0–20, with 0 representing a count of no objects (CCSS.Math.K.CC.A.1).

After creating a performance scale based on the standards in Figure 2.1, the teacher then modifies it to be more student friendly for her five-year-old students. She previously introduced the scale to students, and they have been working on some of the targets for an extended period of time. The teacher makes a conscious effort in every lesson to reference the learning targets and scale for her students. At this point in the instructional sequence, she plans to introduce and briefly explain a new learning target.

Figure 2.1: Elementary Example of a Performance Scale for Kindergarten Mathematics

Elementary – Mathematics Grade: Kindergarten	
Number Names	
(CCSS.Math.K.CC.A.1): Count to 100 by ones and by tens.	
(CCSS.Math.K.CC.A.2): Count forward beginning from a given number within the known sequence (instead of having it begin at 1).	
(CCSS.Math.K.CC.A.3): Write numbers from 0 to 20. Represent a number of objects with a written numeral 0–20 (with 0 representing a count of no objects).	
4.0	Students will be able to: • *Count, write, read*, and *represent* a number of objects through 100

3.0	Students will be able to:
	• *Count forward* beginning from a given number within the known sequence (instead of having to begin at one)
	   – by ones from any number
	   – by tens from any number
	
	• *Represent* a number of objects with a written numeral 0–20 (with 0 representing a count of no objects)

2.0	Students will *recognize* and *recall* specific vocabulary, including:
	• *count, number, ones, sequence, tens*
	
	Students will be able to:
	   – *Count* to 100 by ones
	   – *Count* to 100 by tens
	   – *Write* numbers 0 to 20

1.0	With help, partial success at level 2.0 content and level 3.0 content
0.0	Even with help, no success

Figure 2.2 displays the student-friendly scale the teacher created based on Figure 2.1.

Figure 2.2: Student-Friendly Performance Scale for Kindergarten Mathematics

Elementary – Mathematics	Grade: Kindergarten

Number Names

(**CCSS.Math.K.CC.A.1**): Count to 100 by ones and by tens.

(**CCSS.Math.K.CC.A.2**): Count forward beginning from a given number within the known sequence (instead of having it begin at 1).

(**CCSS.Math.K.CC.A.3**): Write numbers from 0 to 20. Represent a number of objects with a written numeral 0–20 (with 0 representing a count of no objects).

4.0	• **I CAN** count, write, read, and represent numbers through 100.	
3.0	• **I CAN** count forward by ones or tens from any number. • **I CAN** write the number of objects I count.	
2.0	**I KNOW** the following words: *count, number, ones, sequence, tens.* • **I CAN** count to 100 by ones. • **I CAN** count to 100 by tens. • **I CAN** write numbers 0 to 20.	
1.0	• **With help, I CAN** do some of the things above.	

The students are sitting on a rug in front of the board where the student-friendly scale is posted. The teacher introduces her lesson:

> Boys and girls, I want you to think about what we have been doing during math this week and tell your buddy something that you have learned how to do.

The teacher walks quickly through the classroom as the students talk, listening to the conversations to determine how well students understand the targets that have already been introduced and practiced. She then moves back to the front of the group, standing beside the scale.

> Nice job! I heard most of you talking about counting by ones and tens to one hundred, and that is exactly what we have been learning how to do during math time.
>
> Today, we're going to work on a new target: counting objects and writing down the number you count. Let's talk about this picture on the scale and figure out what it means.
>
> *The teacher points to the picture on the scale related to the new target on level 3.0.*
>
> What are these? *The teacher points to the stars in the picture and hears multiple students respond correctly.* That's right. They are stars. Let's count them. *The teacher and students count the stars, and then the teacher points to the equals sign and the numeral 8.* If the picture showed soccer balls, you could count them. If the picture showed hamburgers, you could count them.

In just a few minutes, the teacher reviews the targets from previous lessons and identifies, explains, and connects the learning target for the day to the activity the students will be doing.

Note that the teacher did not "teach" the target. The students discussed the picture representing the learning target to connect what they would be learning to the scale.

Elementary Nonexample of Using Performance Targets and Learning Scales

The nonexample kindergarten teacher is aiming at the same academic standards as the example teacher and has wisely invested the time needed to create a performance scale based on the standard's language as well as a student-friendly scale. He briefly introduces the scale to his students at the beginning of the unit, but has not been intentional and consistent about using the scale to focus students on specific learning targets contained in the learning progression. Feeling a bit guilty about wasting his investment of time on building a scale he has scarcely used, the teacher decides to revisit the scale in the day's lesson. The student-friendly scale is displayed on the board, and the students are seated on the rug. Here is how he begins:

Boys and girls, I want to take a little bit of time to talk with you about our math targets and scale. Which targets have we focused on recently? *One student shares and says they have been working on counting by tens and ones to one hundred.*

Nice job! That is correct. My question today is where do we go from here? What will be the next thing we will learn? *The teacher calls on one student, and he responds by saying they need to count from numbers like thirty-six and forty.*

That is one of the next targets on the scale. Does anyone else want to add anything? *The teacher pauses briefly before continuing.*

Actually we will be working on the other target that is pictured. *The teacher points to the picture of the correct target on the scale.* The next thing you will do is write numbers for the objects you count. Does that make sense? *Students*

> *nod in agreement.* Do you see how we can use the scale to help make sure we learn everything we need to know before moving to first grade? *Students nod again.*
>
> As we continue to work on different learning targets, use the scale to make sure you are learning everything you need to learn. Okay, let's get on with our lesson for today.

This teacher misses the mark in several ways. In his attempt to be brief, he addresses his questions to the whole group and hears thoughts from only one student. The teacher does not guide the students to the next learning target, and his presentation and conversation do not encourage students to make connections between the scale and their learning. He identifies the target and states what they will *do* next, not what they will *learn*. This approach may cause confusion for students since he provides no explanation of the new target. Students might also become anxious if they are having trouble understanding the targets or scale when the teacher tells them to "use the scale to make sure they are learning everything they need to learn." He assumes the silent nods of the students indicate comprehension, but there is no assurance students understand any of the learning targets.

Secondary Example of Using Learning Targets and Performance Scales

This secondary example is focused on three high school biology standards related to cellular structure and function introduced earlier in this guide. Although this figure was previously shown (see Figure V, page 37), it is displayed once again in Figure 2.3. The teacher has created a poster-sized version of the scale, is displaying the scale as a PowerPoint slide and, just to make sure all students have ready access to the scale, handed out copies for students' academic notebooks.

Figure 2.3: Performance Scale for High School Biology Standards

High School – Biology	Grades: Ninth–Twelfth

Cellular Structure and Function

(CPALMS Life Science SC.912.L.14.2): Relate structure to function for the components of plant and animal cells. Explain the role of cell membranes as a highly selective barrier (passive and active transport).

(CPALMS Life Science SC.912.L.14.3): Compare and contrast the general structures of plant and animal cells. Compare and contrast the general structures of prokaryotic and eukaryotic cells.

(CPALMS Life Science SC.912.L.14.4): Compare and contrast structure and function of various types of microscopes.

4.0	Students will be able to: • *Research* ways that cell components are used in medical advancement.
3.0	Students will be able to: • *Compare* and *contrast* the general structures of plant and animal cells. **(SC.912.L.14.3)** • *Generalize* the relationship between the structure and function of the components of plant and animal cells. **(SC.912.L.14.2)** • *Compare* and *contrast* the structures found in prokaryotic cells and eukaryotic cells. **(SC.912.L.14.3)** • *Differentiate* between active and passive transport. **(SC.912.L.14.2)** • *Create* an analogy for the cell membranes as role as a barrier. **(SC.912.L.14.2)** • *Compare* and *construct* structure and function of various types of microscopes. **(SC.912.L.14.4)**
2.0	Students will *recognize* or *recall* specific vocabulary, including: • *plant cells, animal cells, eukaryotic cells, cell membrane (plasma membrane), highly selective barrier, permeable, active transport, passive transport, cell wall, cytoplasm, ribosomes, nucleus, nuclear membrane, nucleolus, chromatic, endoplasmic reticulum, microtubules, microfilaments, vacuoles, mitochondria, Golgi apparatus, chloroplasts, lysosomes, hypotonic, hypertonic, isotonic solutions, component, organelle, chromosomes, phospholipid, polar, molecule, vesicles* In addition, students will *recognize* or *recall* specific affixes: • *cyto-, nuc-, chroma-, micro-, mito-, vac-, chloro-, lyso-, hypo-, hyper-, iso-, pro-, eu-, trans-* Students will be able to: • *Identify* the components of a eukaryotic cell (cell wall, cytoplasm, ribosomes, nucleus, nuclear envelope, nucleolus, chromatic, endoplasmic reticulum, microtubules, microfilaments, vacuoles, mitochondria, Golgi apparatus, chloroplasts, lysosomes). **(SC.912.L.14.3)** • *Describe* the relationship between the structures and functions of the components of plant and animal cells. **(SC.912.L.14.2)** • *Describe* how the cell membrane is a highly selective barrier. **(SC.912.L.14.2)** • *Identify* how materials pass in and out of a cell (passive and active transport). **(SC.912.L.14.2)**
1.0	With help, partial success at level 2.0 content and level 3.0 content
0.0	Even with help, no success

This is the first time the students have seen this teacher-created scale. The teacher begins his lesson this way:

> Today, we are beginning a new unit on cellular structure and function. I have just distributed what is called a performance scale that contains a progression of learning targets for this unit. Don't let the amount of information in the scale overwhelm you. I do not expect you to know any of the information on this scale at this point. We will spend time working on many fascinating activities and labs to help you learn everything that you need to know by the end of the unit.
>
> Level 3.0 lists the learning targets for you to reach by the end of the unit. Let's look at the verbs used for these learning targets. You will see things like comparing and contrasting, generalizing, and creating analogies that will require analytical thinking. But don't worry; we will begin with the simpler thinking in level 2.0 and work our way up the scale. Now look at the verbs at level 2.0. Together we will start by discussing the vocabulary, and then identifying and describing relationships and components of cellular structure and function. When we understand the information at level 2.0 on the scale, we will be ready to move on to the targets at level 3.0.
>
> Once you have accomplished the level 3.0 learning goal targets, you will be given a task for the complex target at level 4.0 that asks you to stretch past the level 3.0 goals and relate what you learned to the field of medicine. Once you understand and can do everything at the other levels of the scale, you will be ready to connect what you have learned with the real-world application task from level 4.0. Think of this scale as a journey we'll take together. The learning targets are mile markers or stops along the way where we'll absorb new information and acquire new thinking processes. We may have to make some rest stops along the way to consolidate what we know before we make the last big push to our final destination, level 4.0.

Secondary Nonexample of Using Learning Targets and Performance Scales

The scenario in the nonexample is similar in many ways to the example. The teacher is focused on the same set of biology standards and presents the same scale to her students, who have never worked with learning targets or goals formatted into a scale before. However, she takes a much different approach than her colleague does. Here is how she begins:

> Today, we are beginning a new unit on cellular structure and function. I have just distributed what is called a scale and learning targets for this unit. From now on, you will get a scale like this one at the beginning of each unit. We will discuss each one of the targets on the scale. Just think about how much information you will learn by the end of the unit.
>
> Let's begin by talking about the list of bullet points you see at level 3.0 on the scale. These bullet points are learning targets that both the state and I would like you to reach by the end of the unit.
>
> *The teacher then begins to explain each target at level 3.0, providing examples to demonstrate what she plans to teach.*
>
> Now, let's look at the bullets, or targets, at level 2.0. These are called foundational targets. You must learn these targets before the ones on level 3.0.
>
> *The teacher then begins going over the vocabulary and each of the targets, explaining unfamiliar terms and providing examples to demonstrate what she plans to teach.*
>
> We will use this scale during the unit to help you understand what you are supposed to learn. You may want to use it as a way to keep tabs on the things you know and what you may need to learn. We will refer to the scale again at the end of class, so you can put your handouts away for now.

In just a minute, you will be watching a video that introduces some of the basic aspects of this topic. Listen carefully and take good notes so you will be ready for the discussion after the video.

You are no doubt as exhausted as the nonexample teacher's students at the cognitive overload she has created. Although the teacher put a lot of effort into this lesson, she made too many of the common mistakes for it to be considered effective.

Determining If Students Understand the Scale and Its Targets

Monitoring to determine whether students understand the learning targets and what the scale means requires effort from both the students and the teacher. Students need to demonstrate behaviors that indicate they understand the goals, scale, and progression of learning. Teachers need to verify who has reached this desired result and react accordingly, providing guidance or clarification as needed. Here are some specific examples of monitoring the implementation of learning goals and scales:

- Students draw pictures or diagrams to explain the learning goal or target for a given lesson. While students are working, the teacher walks around the classroom and scans the artifacts, asking questions where needed to ensure that students know what the targets are.

- Students work in small groups on learning scenarios the teacher provides that ask them to identify the missing piece of critical content and the related learning target that caused the gap in learning and prevented the student in the scenario from achieving the goal. The teacher listens to students' conversations as they discuss the relationship between the foundational targets and the learning goal targets on the scale to determine what piece is missing.

- The teacher provides students the name of one of the activities or tasks that were implemented over a given period of time in their classroom and asks them to write a brief description of how the activity or task relates to the learning goal or target. The teacher reads over the descriptions to verify students understand the given relationship for their assigned activity.

- The teacher gives students a list of all of the activities or tasks that were implemented over a given period of time in their classroom and asks them to work with a partner to sort them by the learning target they align with, and then explain where and how each one fits in the progression of learning required to achieve the target goal. The teacher walks through the classroom, observing partners as they sort the tasks and listening as they discuss the progression of knowledge, taking note of who can identify the progression accurately.

The student proficiency scale in Table 2.1 will help you assess whether your students are demonstrating an understanding of the learning targets and their progression on the performance scale as you implement this technique.

Table 2.1: Student Proficiency Scale for Using Targets and Scales

Emerging	Fundamental	Desired Result
Students provide responses regarding the learning targets and scale progression.	Students provide accurate responses regarding the learning targets and scale progression.	Students provide comprehensive, accurate responses regarding the learning targets and scale progression.
Students provide responses indicating they recognize their current activities and tasks relate to the learning goal or target.	Students can explain how some of their current activities and tasks relate to the scale and its targets.	Students can explain how their current activities and tasks relate to the learning goal targets and to the progression of learning.
Students can identify individual targets on the scale.	Students can identify the learning progression embedded in the scale, from simple to complex, between targets.	Students can explain the learning progression embedded in the scale, from simple to complex, between targets.

Scaffold and Extend Instruction to Meet Students' Needs

Determining whether your students understand the targets, goals, learning progression, and scale will get easier with practice. You will soon recognize the signs that indicate a student or group of students need redirection, support, or enrichment. The following suggestions are meant to be demonstrative. They should provide some ideas for you to springboard from.

Scaffolding

- If students struggle with identifying the relationship between the current activity and its aligned goal, provide clues that walk them through the highlights of the activity or task and ask what they learned from the task. Write down the things they say to help them visualize the connection between the goal and activity.

- Before having students verbally explain the learning goal or target for the lesson, allow them time to turn to a neighbor to discuss the key points and "borrow ideas" to use in their explanation.

- For students whose artifacts or work do not demonstrate that they can identify the progression of knowledge between the targets in the scale, provide an exemplar or worked example from another student that does demonstrate the progression and ask students to compare and contrast the two works. Have them discuss what they notice and what they can do to adjust their artifact or work to make it align with the exemplar.

- For students having difficulty understanding the difference between the related targets from different levels of the scale, provide more explicit instruction using examples to demonstrate the different expectations at each level. Ask students to research the verbs used in the targets and discuss the difference between each of the verbs.

Extending

- Ask students to analyze how specific activities contribute to the overall learning and understanding of the target.

- Ask students to compare and contrast all of the foundational and learning goal targets in the scale and rank them according to their importance in developing the understanding necessary to reach the cognitively complex targets.

USING STUDENT-FRIENDLY SCALES

The techniques thus far have featured targets and scales containing the precise wording of the academic standards. Using this approach ensures that the targets and scales remain aligned with the rigor or cognitive complexity of the standard. However, when this process is followed, scales contain exclusively "teacher-friendly language." Teacher-created scales can be used with older elementary students and grade levels above because these students are able to read and understand the targets and scales as created. However, learning targets and scales are only powerful if students truly comprehend what they are expected to know and do. For many students, the wording of the targets and expectations for each performance level of the scale might need to be explained and then translated into student-friendly language to make the learning experience meaningful. Just as with teacher-created scales, student-friendly scales are ideally created by teams of teachers working together. For younger learners unable to read with understanding and students with special needs, the teacher can rephrase, shorten, or visually demonstrate the learning targets and scale using student-friendly language to make the content and learning trajectory more accessible.

How to Effectively Use Student-Friendly Scales

There are two groups of students who will benefit from the creation of student-friendly scales: 1) students who are able to read on grade level but will have difficulty understanding the challenging academic vocabulary of a teacher-created scale and 2) very young students or students with special needs whose reading skills need a great deal of support.

Students Who Can Read but Need More Student-Friendly Vocabulary

One way to create a student-friendly scale for students who are able to read and write but are having difficulty understanding the challenging academic language used in a teacher-created scale or the requirements for mastery of the targets is to involve the students in revising the language of the scale. After the teacher-created scale has been presented, invite the students to discuss and rewrite the content for levels 2.0, 3.0, and 4.0 using language they understand. Students could work individually or in small groups to reword the targets on each scale level and then share their revisions with the class. Care should be taken to ensure that the student translations maintain the level of cognitive complexity the standard requires. With guidance from the teacher, the class as a whole can then create and approve a student-friendly version that includes specific, well-defined examples that model what students must imitate to demonstrate competence at each level of the scale.

Younger Students and Students With Special Needs

Very young students or those with special needs require a different approach because they have limited background knowledge and reading and writing skills. If your students require this approach, revise and rephrase a scale for them. Consider the following guidelines when creating student-friendly scales for these students.

Preserve the Intent of the Standard

Take care when adapting the scale to select words that students can understand. However, guard against changing the intent of the standard. In other words, if the standard requires the student to *demonstrate,* choose simpler replacement words such as *show* or *use.* These more familiar words convey the same level of thinking and intention and are appropriate replacements. Conversely, the word *demonstrate* should not be replaced with the word *name.* Even though both words might be on the same level of processing (retrieval), they are very different operations. Refer to the New Taxonomy (Figure N, page 27) to ensure the action verbs you select as replacements in student-friendly targets and scales require the same level of cognitively complex thinking and operation from students as those originally stated in the standard.

Include Words Essential to Demonstrating the Standard

You may consider asking the following questions when creating student-friendly targets from academic standards:

- Is the word essential to demonstrating the standard? If so, should you include it in the student-friendly scale?

- For nonessential words, what other words can you select that have the same meaning but are student friendly?

Words essential to demonstrating the standard's intent, such as the action verbs *identify, compare,* and *count*, and crucial vocabulary, such as *circle, line,* and *key details*, should be retained to avoid watering down the standard. Use this opportunity to introduce terms and define new terms to deepen students' academic vocabularies. You are the ultimate arbiter for determining which terms to share with students or which to recast in student-friendly language. Always retain the intent of the learning target or scale.

Kindergarten standards often require students to *decompose* numbers. To avoid the unpleasant connotations of this word, which are clearly not the intent of the standard's word choice here, ask students to *break down* or *break apart* numbers instead. Young students might find it difficult to understand the phrase *participate in collaborative conversations with diverse partners* as required in the first Speaking and Listening Common Core English Language Arts standard. As long as you ensure that students work with a variety of partners, the phrase could be replaced with *talk with your buddy.* It is up to you to make sure your students ultimately understand the intention and meaning behind the words used in the standard.

Use the I CAN Sentence Starter

Use the I CAN phrase as a simple sentence starter to preface learning targets. I CAN statements help students concentrate on the immediate goal at hand as well as encourage them to take ownership of a learning target. Stiggins et al. (2006) believe that beginning each target with an approachable phrase, such as I CAN, encourages students to understand and measure their own learning and progress. Both students and the teacher can use I CAN statements to formatively assess mastery of the content.

Add Visual Support

Student-friendly pictures add to the sense of community and foster engagement. Many students are able to connect with the words on a scale more quickly when a visual image is added. Visual aids emphasize without speaking or reading and are often used as a prereading strategy to activate prior knowledge. Rao and Gagie (2006) discuss how visual supports specifically help children with autism, but all students will benefit from photos, clip art, or even simple teacher- or student-drawn images. Visuals will attract and hold attention, enable students to focus on the message, and make abstract concepts more concrete. Visual supports can increase the understanding of language, while providing the structure needed to clarify expectations and targets. When selecting and preparing images or graphics to add visual support in a scale, follow these tips:

- Determine what will be written and what will be visual.

- Make sure the images reinforce, illustrate, or provide examples related to the target.

- To avoid confusion, use only one image per main idea.

- Do not use a graphic that is too crowded in detail.

Once Created, Explain the Teacher-Created, Student-Friendly Scale

Part of what makes a scale student friendly for younger learners is the support the teacher provides to ensure understanding of the expectations required at each level of the scale. If the scale includes both written and visual explanations, the teacher simply needs to add the auditory or verbal piece that connects everything. This combination of written, visual, and verbal support should help ensure that students understand what the targets and scale mean.

Common Mistakes

Creating student-friendly scales and making learning targets and the progression of learning more understandable to students requires thoughtful contemplation to ensure the underlying aim of the standard remains true. You must ensure that the quest for graphics or images does not become the end in itself. Remember that the power behind the scale may be lost if you develop an ineffective student-friendly scale. The most common mistakes to avoid when creating student-friendly scales include those in the previous chapter for teacher-created scales as well as the following:

- The teacher does not ensure that student-generated examples accurately illustrate the expectations for each level of the learning progression in the student-friendly scale and are incorporated into the revised version of the student-friendly scale.

- The teacher does not correctly translate or help the students translate the intent of the standard to student-friendly language.

- The teacher uses a generic scale that does not describe the specific content targets.

- The teacher creates an effective student-friendly scale but does not use it to provide direction and structure for classroom learning.

Examples and Nonexamples of Using Student-Friendly Scales

Following are examples and nonexamples of using student-friendly scales in classrooms. As you read, verify the intent or power of the standard and the original teacher-created learning targets and performance scale have not been distorted during the revision process. Determine that even though the wording or examples are simplified, the revised content is accurate. Consider the common mistakes mentioned previously and note how the example teachers avoid them.

Elementary Example of Using Student-Friendly Scales

The learning targets for this elementary example of using student-friendly scales are unpacked from the standards in Figure 3.1.

Figure 3.1: Student-Friendly Performance Scale for Kindergarten Mathematics

Elementary – Mathematics	Grade: Kindergarten

Number Names

(CCSS.Math.K.CC.A.1): Count to 100 by ones and by tens.

(CCSS.Math.K.CC.A.2): Count forward beginning from a given number within the known sequence (instead of having it begin at 1).

(CCSS.Math.K.CC.A.3): Write numbers from 0 to 20. Represent a number of objects with a written numeral 0–20 (with 0 representing a count of no objects).

4.0	• **I CAN** count, write, read, and represent numbers through 100.
3.0	• **I CAN** count forward by ones or tens from any number. • **I CAN** write the number of objects I count.
2.0	**I KNOW** the following words: *count, number, ones, sequence, tens.* • **I CAN** count to 100 by ones. • **I CAN** count to 100 by tens. • **I CAN** write numbers 0 to 20.
1.0	• **With help, I CAN** do some of the things above.

Note that the teacher has used I CAN statements to motivate her students to focus on the learning targets and embrace them as their own learning goals. Note that in level 3.0, the teacher has changed the original language of the standard from *represent a number of objects with a written numeral* to *I CAN write the number of objects I count.* She has also translated the standard's language *count forward beginning from a given number within the known sequence (instead of having it begin at 1)* to *I CAN count forward by ones or tens from any number.*

The teacher has prepared a poster-sized version of the performance scale in Figure 3.1 and anchored it on her easel. She signals her students to leave their tables and chairs and seat themselves in their assigned spots on the teaching rug at the rear of the classroom. Here is how she begins her lesson introducing the student-friendly performance scale:

> Boys and girls, quickly get into your looking and listening position. Eyes up on the easel. I want you to look carefully at all of the different words and pictures you see on the poster there. See if you can read any words or recognize any of the pictures. Here's my question for you: What do you think we are going to learn about today? Don't shout out any answers. I want you to quietly answer my question in your mind. I see smiles on some faces. Talk to your buddy about what we are going to learn today.

Students talk about numbers, math, and counting.

> Good thinking, boys and girls. This poster is going to help us keep track of all of the things we learn about math and numbers and counting this year. Notice that on this side of the poster, there are words that tell all of the things you'll know and do. *The teacher runs her hand along the left-hand side of the poster.* On this side of the poster, there are pictures that show you what the words mean (*the teacher runs her hand along the right-hand side of the poster*). From now on, every

time we work on math, we are going to find out exactly where we are on the poster. One of my favorite parts of the poster is the picture of a teacher helping a student. The words say: **With help, I CAN do some of the things above.** So, we are all going to climb to the top of the scale, and we will all help each other learn.

Elementary Nonexample of Using Student-Friendly Scales

The nonexample teacher takes some huge shortcuts in creating a student-friendly scale. Although she is working on the same math standards, the scale she creates is not tied to any specific academic standard or content and therefore does not demonstrate a progression of learning. It contains four levels: 1) I need help, 2) I can do some, 3) I can do it all, and 4) I can teach others. Smiley faces provide the visual information to accompany the statements. Informal scales such as these are an excellent monitoring tool that could be used for student self-assessment purposes or as a quick check of student understanding. However, since they do not provide the specific targets that describe competency levels, you cannot use them to track student progress or measure proficiency with the content. In the student-friendly scale example, specific content targets that build toward and ultimately exceed proficiency are detailed at each level in the progression of learning. Visual cues or graphics are added to support and provide connections to the rephrased targets. The critical content that is pulled from the standard is reworded using simple language and I CAN statements to provide direction and communicate the purpose of instruction.

Secondary Example of Using Student-Friendly Scales

The standard that is the focus in this middle school English language arts class is in Figure 3.2. In the following example, the teacher intentionally plans to have students translate and rewrite the 3.0 learning targets from the teacher-created scale to initiate the creation of a student-friendly version of the scale.

Figure 3.2: Teacher-Created Performance Scale for Middle School Reading

(TEKS ELAR 6.11): Reading/Comprehension of Informational Text/Persuasive Text
Students analyze, make inferences, and draw conclusions about persuasive text and provide evidence from text to support their analysis. Students are expected to:
(A) compare and contrast the structure and viewpoints of two different authors writing for the same purpose, noting the stated claim and supporting evidence; and
(B) identify simple faulty reasoning used in persuasive texts.

4.0	Students will be able to: • **Make** and **defend** a decision about which of two persuasive texts written for the same purpose by different authors provides the best or most beneficial information.

3.0	Students will be able to:
	• **Analyze, make inferences,** and **draw conclusions** about persuasive text and provide evidence from the text to support their analysis as they:
	  – **Compare** and **contrast** the structure used by two authors writing for the same purpose, noting the stated claim and supporting evidence
	  – **Compare** and **contrast** the viewpoints of two authors writing for the same purpose, noting the stated claim and supporting evidence

2.0	Students will **recognize** or **recall** specific vocabulary, including: • *faulty reasoning, overgeneralization, illogical conclusion, personal bias, author's purpose, stated purpose, implied purpose, viewpoint, persuasive technique* Students will be able to: • **Use** reading strategies to support interpretation of texts • **Identify** a stated claim • **Identify** simple faulty reasoning used in persuasive texts • **Identify** the structure of a text (sequence, compare and contrast, cause and effect, problem and solution, and description) • **Describe** how authors use structure and viewpoint to influence attitudes, emotions, or actions of a specific audience • **Explain** the effectiveness of the persuasive techniques based on audience, purpose, and message
1.0	With help, partial success at level 2.0 content and level 3.0 content
0.0	Even with help, no success

The student-friendly scale will be posted beside the teacher-created scale, and as the progression of learning moves forward, all the targets will eventually be rewritten in language that students can understand to provide clearer expectations of what they need to learn and do to be successful with the content. This type of activity can be completed with elementary through high school students any time after a teacher-created scale has been introduced and explained to the class.

The teacher introduces his lesson as follows:

> Good morning, class. Today we will spend a little time talking about the learning goal target for our unit of interpreting persuasive texts. Yesterday, I introduced two different documents about zoos. One was an article, and the other was a blog post, but they both provided information about zoos and painted a picture as you read. Our learning goal target for the unit is for you to be able to compare and contrast two different texts, focusing on the structure and the author's viewpoint of the piece.
>
> I want you to spend some time in your small groups talking about the 3.0 learning targets on the scale. I want you to discuss your understanding of the targets and what you think you are expected to do to show that you can compare and contrast two persuasive texts. Then, I want you to put the targets written at level 3.0 in the scale into your own words. When every group has had time to discuss and reword the targets, I will ask everyone to share, and then together as a class we will create a student-friendly version of the 3.0 learning goal targets. You can refer to this version as often as needed to ensure you understand what you are expected to learn and do in this unit. Feel free to refer to the documents introduced yesterday in class or use them as examples as you write.

The teacher guides and supports the student discussion and revisions as needed, staying vigilant to ensure the cognitive integrity of the standard and original targets transfer to the newly created student-friendly version.

Notice in this example that the teacher does not ask the students to revise every target. As the lessons build throughout the unit, the teacher asks students to revise each of the targets and add them to the student-friendly classroom scale posted at the front of the room. The final version of the student-friendly scale with every teacher-created target reworded by students is in Figure 3.3.

Figure 3.3: Student-Friendly Performance Scale for Interpreting Persuasive Texts

	Interpreting Persuasive Texts
4.0	I will be able to: • **_Make_** and **_defend_**—Choose which story is better or makes the most sense and tell how I made my decision.
3.0	I will be able to: • **_Analyze_** (study in detail) and **_determine_** answers to questions using the words from the text as proof as I: — **_Compare_** and **_contrast_** (find similarities and differences between) two stories that were written about the same issue (like the article and blog post I read on zoos). I will look at the <u>structure</u> (the way the story is written) and the author's <u>viewpoint</u> (opinion or position) and think about how both authors made me feel or think about the issue.
2.0	I will be able to: • **_Identify_** the <u>claim</u> (suggestion or argument) made by the author • **_Identify_** the <u>faulty reasoning</u> (flawed logic) in persuasive texts (texts written to convince me to agree with the author's position on an issue) • **_Identify_** the <u>structure</u> (the way the story is written) • **_Describe_** how or talk or write about how the way a story is written and the author's opinion or position have an impact on how I feel or react • **_Explain_** or talk or write about how good a job the author did to persuade me (convince me) to agree with him
1.0	With help, partial success at level 2.0 content and level 3.0 content
0.0	Even with help, no success

Secondary Nonexample of Using Student-Friendly Scales

The same teacher-created scale has previously been shared with students in the following nonexample, and the teacher has the same ultimate goal for the students—to revise the teacher-created scale into a student-friendly version. The teacher introduces her lesson as follows:

> I previously introduced the targets and scale for this unit. Today, you are going to spend time in small groups talking about the learning targets on the scale. You should discuss your understanding of the targets and expectations at each of the scale levels, and then rewrite them in your own words. Once finished, you will listen as others share their student-friendly versions. Listen closely and compare what you have written to what other students have written. Feel free to make changes to your version of the scale if you hear something that makes the target clearer for you.

It is not evident that the teacher plans to involve herself in the revision process at all. She gives the students free rein to revise the language of the original scale and create a simpler version of the targets in their own words. When finished, they only had to compare their creation to other student versions. The teacher did not mention creating examples to provide a clear illustration of expectations, nor did she mention working collaboratively to create an accurate class version that could be used as a reference when needed for clarification purposes. In addition, she asks students to reword targets that have not been explained in detail, and therefore the activity itself compromises the intent of student-friendly scales. In the secondary example, students were asked to work on only a "chunk" of the scale or just the targets at level 3.0. This approach provides more focus and structure and will not overwhelm the students, unlike the approach of the nonexample teacher. Creating a student-friendly version of the learning target as the need unfolds in the progression of learning is a much better use of instructional time and results in a much more accurate version of a student-friendly scale.

Determining If Students Understand the Student-Friendly Scale

A successful student-friendly scale is one that communicates the targets and learning progression simply, clearly, and accurately. An effective revision or translation helps students connect to the language and fosters student understanding of the content targets and performance expectations. You will know whether you achieved the desired result only if you ask your students to engage in an activity that requires them to demonstrate their understanding of the learning targets and scale progression and you monitor or witness this activity by watching, listening, scanning, reviewing, or some other form of observation. Consider the following suggestions when determining whether a student-friendly scale facilitates awareness of the targets, goal, and learning progression.

- Ask students to discuss their understanding of the targets and the performance levels on the scale with a partner. Circulate and listen to the conversations between partners to discover possible misinterpretations, and clarify as needed.

- As students revise targets in their own words, scan student work looking for revised wording that correlates accurately to the level of rigor the standard and original teacher-created targets require.

- Ask questions associated with the targets at different levels of the scale progression and have students hold up two, three, or four cards or fingers to denote the level the question addresses. Watch during the response time to determine which students or which targets might be confused or less clear.

Use the student proficiency scale in Table 3.1 for student-friendly scales to determine whether your students are demonstrating the desired results while using the translated version of the learning targets and scale.

Table 3.1: Student Proficiency Scale for Student-Friendly Scales

Emerging	Fundamental	Desired Result
Students provide responses to simplify the language of the targets when transforming the teacher-created scale to a student-friendly scale.	Students provide responses that accurately simplify the language of the targets while remaining at the same level of cognition when transforming the teacher-created scale to a student-friendly scale.	Students provide responses that accurately and comprehensively simplify the language of the targets while remaining at the same level of cognition and include illustrated examples at each level of the scale when transforming the teacher-created scale to a student-friendly scale.
Students can discuss parts of the student-friendly scale's targets and progression of learning.	Students can describe the student-friendly scale's targets and progression of learning.	Students can describe the relationship between the student-friendly scale's targets and progression of learning.
Student understanding of the learning targets, goal, and what the scale means is sometimes inaccurate and incomplete.	Student understanding of the learning targets, goal, and what the scale means is accurate but sometimes incomplete.	Student understanding of the learning targets, goal, and what the scale means is accurate and all-inclusive.

Scaffold and Extend Instruction to Meet Students' Needs

At times you may need to make adaptations to the creation or implementation process of student-friendly scales. Some students may need more support than simply translating the language used in the targets and scale, while others might require extensions or enhancements to expand learning with the student-friendly scale. The ways in which you support or extend the use of student-friendly scales depend on whether they are teacher created or student revised, as well as the background knowledge, reading, and writing skills of the students involved. Use the following sample adaptations as a springboard for developing other approaches to meet your students' needs.

Scaffolding

- For older students who struggle with the process of translating or revising targets on a teacher-created scale, provide resources (e.g., dictionary, thesaurus, computers) or a template with guiding questions to assist students as they work together to create simpler targets at the same level of rigor as the teacher-created scale.

- Highlight words or post only the target from the scale to be covered during the lesson to prevent overwhelming students and aid in discussions.

- Ask students to draw or represent the targets, learning expectations, and big ideas nonlinguistically for each level of the scale.

Extending

- Ask students to compare similarities and differences of group interpretations of the teacher-created targets and scale and then explain which translation they think is best, justifying their reasoning.

- Ask students to share visual representations or diagrams of the goal and targets to add to the posted version of the student-friendly scale.

- Ask students to compare the student-friendly version of the scale to the academic learning standard or teacher-created scale and create a crosswalk document explaining the translation between the two.

USING STUDENT-GENERATED SCALES

One way to heighten your students' engagement and immersion in the content is to have them develop individual learning targets and scales. Students become more invested in their learning process when they can relate a personal interest to the compulsory learning goal targets. The personal connection encourages active participation in the learning process, inspires diligence and perseverance with the subject matter, and empowers students to become independent learners. Being allowed to exercise some control over their own learning fosters personal efficacy and student self-direction. According to Hom and Murphy (1983), "A growing body of research indicates that when students are working on goals they themselves have set, they are more motivated and efficient, and they achieve more than they do when working on goals that have been set by the teacher." Therefore, having students develop personal goals related to the targets on the teacher-created scale supports the development of autonomous learning, thereby strengthening their propensity to learn. Use caution before you enthusiastically embrace this technique: It necessitates a deep understanding of targets and scales.

How to Effectively Use Student-Generated Scales

Keep the following steps in mind as you plan for students to effectively create and implement student-generated targets or goals and performance scales that promote independent learning.

Step 1: Teacher Introduces and Explains Learning Targets and Performance Scales

For students to personalize their learning, they need a thorough understanding of the learning targets and learning trajectory of the content or unit of instruction. Connections between the learning targets and how the content is applied in the real world should be made by the teacher to initiate student thinking about the content that will be covered. During this presentation of the learning targets, encourage students to look for connections between their personal interests and the content to determine a possible area, theme, or related concept they would like to learn more about.

Step 2: Student Identifies Personal Learning Goal Target

Once the teacher-created targets and scale have been shared, students should be given time to generate a learning goal that is personally important and related to the content. The individual target or goal the students create should be aligned with the learning target(s) at level 3.0 of the teacher-created scale. Some students might be able to quickly establish a connection they want to pursue. Others might be unable to identify anything that piques their curiosity, so you might consider providing time for research or reflection. Conversations that encourage students to think about their own learning and challenge them to articulate a personal relationship to the content may be helpful. Establishing the personal target could be postponed until the students have had a little exposure to the content, if preferred.

A structured organizer, such as a KWHL table (What do I know? What do I want to find out? How will I learn it? What have I learned or do I still want to learn?), may be helpful to the students during the initial brainstorming or development process. Another approach is to have students answer guiding questions pertaining to the targets at level 3.0 on the teacher-created scale such as the following:

- What are some things I am interested in right now that are related to the topic?

- What do I want to better understand during this unit of study?

Once students determine their personal learning targets, they should write them using the same format or language from the teacher-created scale (e.g., I will be able to . . . or I will . . .) to promote a sense of personal ownership of their learning. A discussion may be required to explain that personal learning targets must maintain the cognitive intent of the original learning target to ensure similar actions or levels of thinking are apparent in the personalized goals. Examples of student-generated personal learning goal targets are in Figure 4.1. Notice how the boldfaced verbs in the level 3.0 learning target goals in the teacher-created scale are repeated in the student-generated learning goal targets.

Figure 4.1: Student-Generated Personal Learning Goal Targets

3.0 Learning Goal Target From Teacher-Created Learning Goal Target	3.0 Learning Goal Target From Student-Generated Target
(C3 Framework. D2.Civ.12.3-5, National Council for the Social Studies)	
Explain how rules and laws change society and how people change rules and laws.	I will **explain how** new rules have changed the game of basketball and find out which players caused the rule changes.
(CCSS.Math.7.RP.A.2)	
Recognize and **represent** proportional relationships between quantities.	I will **recognize** the proportional relationships evident in the human body and learn how to **represent** them accurately when I draw.
(CCSS.ELA-Literacy.RI.8.6)	
The student will **determine** an author's point of view or purpose in a text and **analyze** how the author acknowledges and responds to conflicting evidence or viewpoints.	I will **analyze** a favorite author's life and background to **determine** what impact his or her life experiences might have had on the way he or she writes.

Step 3: Student Generates a Personalized Scale

Now that your students have identified their personal learning targets that are aligned to level 3.0 of the teacher-created scale, they are ready to build a personalized scale. This process closely follows the one teachers use to create a scale. Since the level 3.0 targets have been identified, the next step is for the students to consider what they will need to learn or do to be able to reach their personal goal. Once determined, this information should be added to the foundational level 2.0 of their personalized scales. The content contained at level 2.0 of the teacher-created scale should also be incorporated, but it may be modified slightly to associate it more closely with the personalized student targets. Specific actions or independent research required to build the background knowledge necessary to achieve the student goal should also be included at level 2.0 of the student-generated scale.

Once the foundational targets have been aligned with the students' personal goals, they are ready to consider a personal level 4.0 target. Again, it should relate to the level 4.0 target on the teacher-created scale but may be personalized to deepen and enhance the identified student targets. When complete, the student-generated scale becomes a personalized plan of action that, if followed, will lead students to their selected learning destination.

Step 4: Teacher Reviews, Supports, and Guides

Review all student-generated scales to ensure they are aligned to both the content and the cognitive complexity of the targets on the teacher-created scale. Throughout this process, provide support and guidance to facilitate a learning environment that promotes independence. Resources, both print and electronic, should be available to encourage and sustain personalized learning. The perspectives and interests reflected in the students' individualized learning targets should be interwoven where possible in the learning process. Students should feel both challenged and supported while developing and deepening the thinking necessary to attain their self-assigned goals. Time for reflection must be provided for students to connect their classroom learning to their personalized goals.

Varied levels of support and guidance might be required to assist students in this process. Some students may need direction from beginning to end of the personalized learning journey. Others may only need time to reflect, focus, and self-monitor to reach their goals. The use of student-generated targets and scales in the classroom requires teachers to act as both facilitator and mentor as they champion the students on their personalized learning journeys.

Common Mistakes

The most common mistakes to avoid when working with student-generated scales include the following:

- The teacher does not explain the teacher-created scale or learning targets with enough detail or clarity for students to determine worthwhile personalized goals related to the content.

- The teacher does not verify the student-generated learning targets and scale are aligned with the cognitive complexity of the target(s) on the teacher-created or student-friendly scale.

- The teacher does not review the student-generated targets and scale for validity and connection to the content, eventually causing students to become discouraged about their progress with independent learning.

- The teacher does not provide essential support or time for reflection during the generation or implementation process to ensure students remain invested in their personalized learning.

Examples and Nonexamples of Using Student-Generated Scales

The following examples and nonexamples demonstrate the use of student-generated scales in the classroom. Although the content and grade levels may differ from yours, identify the ways the example teachers are effectively using student-generated scales with her students and the common mistakes made by the nonexample teachers.

Elementary Example of Using Student-Generated Scales

The elementary example showing the use of student-generated scales in the classroom is focused on the following fifth-grade science standard: *The student will investigate and understand how sound is created and transmitted, and how it is used* (VA Science SOL 5.2 a, b, c, and d). In preparation for asking her students to create a personalized learning target based on this standard, the teacher has created a performance scale based on the standard. The scale is in Figure 4.2.

Figure 4.2: Teacher-Created Performance Scale for Elementary Science

Elementary – Science	Grade: Fifth

(VA Science SOL 5.2 a, b, c, d): The student will investigate and understand how sound is created and transmitted, and how it is used. Key concepts include:
- compression waves
- vibration, compression, wavelength, frequency, amplitude
- the ability of different media (solids, liquids, and gases) to transmit sound
- uses and applications of sound waves

4.0	Students will be able to: • ***Devise*** one sound source that transmits multiple frequencies, ***justify*** how the frequencies are created and transmitted, and ***explain*** how the sound source could be used
3.0	Students will be able to: • ***Investigate*** how sound is created and transmitted • ***Investigate*** how sound is used
2.0	Students ***will recognize*** or ***recall*** specific vocabulary, including: • *compression waves, vibration, compression, wavelength, frequency, amplitude, sound waves* Students will be able to: • ***Analyze*** how sound is created and transmitted and how it is used – ***Apply*** knowledge of sound to form conclusions • ***Understand*** how sound is created and transmitted and how it is used – ***Explain how*** sound is created and transmitted – ***Identify*** and ***explain*** the ability of different media (solids, liquids, and gases) to transmit sound – ***Identify*** and ***explain*** the uses and applications of sound waves – ***Describe*** the relationship between vibration, compression, wavelength, frequency, and amplitude and the creation and transmission of sound
1.0	With help, partial success at level 2.0 content and level 3.0 content
0.0	Even with help, no success

The teacher has introduced the scale that he created and explained it to his students. The teacher also develops a template that provides a structure for the scale students will generate based on their personalized learning target. Figure 4.3 shows the template. Note how the teacher has divided the scale into two parts: a teacher-created scale on the left-hand side of the figure and a column for the student-generated scale on the right-hand side.

The teacher introduces his lesson as follows:

> Class, we've been studying how sound is created and transmitted for several days. We've done a number of activities related to the various learning targets on our performance scale. We've had some very interesting discussions about this standard and its various applications in the real world. My question for you is this: What are some things related to how sound is created and transmitted that you are interested in learning more about?

The students brainstorm possible topics with partners and then share their ideas with the class. After time for reflection and research, students are asked to document their chosen personalized learning targets on the template shown in Figure 4.3.

Figure 4.3: Template for Student-Generated Scale

Middle School – Science   Grade: Fifth

(VA Science SOL 5.2 a, b, c, d): The student will investigate and understand how sound is created and transmitted, and how it is used. Key concepts include:

- compression waves
- vibration, compression, wavelength, frequency, amplitude
- the ability of different media (solids, liquids, and gases) to transmit sound
- uses and applications of sound waves

Level	Teacher-Created Performance Scale	Student–Generated Scale
4.0	Students will be able to: • **Devise** one sound source that transmits multiple frequencies, **justify** how the frequencies are created and transmitted, and **discuss** how the sound source could be used	**I will devise** one sound source that transmits different multiple **frequencies**, **justify** how the frequencies are created and transmitted, and **discuss** how the sound source could be used
3.0	Students will be able to: • **Investigate** how sound is created and transmitted • **Investigate** how sound is used	**I will achieve all of the 3.0 targets on the teacher scale to achieve my personalized learning target below and:**

2.0	Students **will recognize** or **recall** specific vocabulary, including:
	• *compression waves, vibration, compression, wavelength, frequency, amplitude, sound waves*
	Students will be able to:
	• **Analyze** how sound is created and transmitted and how it is used
	  – **Apply** knowledge of sound to form conclusions
	• **Understand** how sound is created and transmitted and how it is used
	  – **Explain** how sound is created and transmitted
	  – **Identify** and **explain** the ability of different media (solids, liquids, and gases) to transmit sound
	  – **Identify** and **explain** the uses and applications of sound waves
	  – **Describe the relationship** between vibration, compression, wavelength, frequency, and amplitude and the creation and transmission of sound
		I will achieve all of the 2.0 targets on the teacher scale to achieve my personalized learning target.
		
		Additional vocabulary or targets required:

1.0	With help, partial success at level 2.0 content and level 3.0 content	
0.0	Even with help, no understanding demonstrated	

Here is how she explains the process:

> Now that you have had time to determine a topic that interests you related to our study of sound and how it is transmitted, I would like you to create a personal learning target for level 3.0 that matches the difficulty level of the 3.0 targets on the teacher-created scale.
>
> Let me model for you how you might accomplish this. To do this, I will need a volunteer to help me. The volunteer needs to already have in mind the topic he or she will use to personalize his or her student-generated scale.

A student volunteers, and the teacher determines that Madison's topic is guitars. The teacher displays the side-by-side template on her whiteboard and hands a marker to Madison.

> Now, look carefully at the two learning goal targets at level 3.0. Think about your topic, guitars, and figure out what your personalized goal might sound like. You can use some of the same words as I used in my teacher-created scale.

Madison begins to write her learning target in the right-hand column of the student-generated scale: *I will investigate how guitars create and transmit sound.*

> Excellent thinking, Madison.

Several other students have their hands raised as if to volunteer to write their personalized learning targets. The teacher directs them to get into their work groups to help each other select a topic and write a personalized learning target for level 3.0.

In a subsequent lesson, the teacher explains and models how students can generate a level 2.0 target that will help them understand a key prerequisite for achieving their level 3.0 learning target. Likewise, the teacher guides and models for students how to create a level 4.0 learning target. Figure 4.4 illustrates a student-generated scale with personalized learning targets for levels 2.0, 3.0, and 4.0. Note that students are required to commit to achieving all of the teacher-created scale targets in addition to achieving their personalized learning target.

Figure 4.4: Student-Generated Performance Scale With Personalized Learning Targets

Middle School – Science	Grade: Fifth

(VA Science SOL 5.2 a, b, c, d): The student will investigate and understand how sound is created and transmitted, and how it is used. Key concepts include:
- compression waves
- vibration, compression, wavelength, frequency, amplitude
- the ability of different media (solids, liquids, and gases) to transmit sound
- uses and applications of sound waves

Level	Teacher-Created Performance Scale	Student-Generated Scale
4.0	Students will be able to: • **Devise** one sound source that transmits multiple frequencies, **justify** how the frequencies are created and transmitted, and **discuss** how the sound source could be used	**I will devise** one sound source that transmits different multiple frequencies, **justify** how the frequencies are created and transmitted, and **discuss** how the sound source could be used. • I will build a five-string guitar, explain how different pitches are created and transmitted, and play a song to show how my sound source is used.
3.0	Students will be able to: • **Investigate** how sound is created and transmitted • **Investigate** how sound is used	**I will achieve all of the 3.0 targets on the teacher scale to achieve my personalized learning target below and:** • I will investigate how guitars create and transmit sound.

2.0	Students **will recognize** or **recall** specific vocabulary, including: • *compression waves, vibration, compression, wavelength, frequency, amplitude, sound waves* Students will be able to: • **Analyze** how sound is created and transmitted and how it is used – **Apply** knowledge of sound to form conclusions • **Understand** how sound is created and transmitted and how it is used – **Explain how** sound is created and transmitted – **Identify** and **explain** the ability of different media (solids, liquids, and gases) to transmit sound – **Identify and explain** the uses and applications of sound waves – **Describe the relationship** between vibration, compression, wavelength, frequency and amplitude and the creation and transmission of sound	**I will achieve all of the 2.0 targets on the teacher scale to achieve my personalized learning target.** **Additional vocabulary or targets required:** • I will understand how guitars create and transmit sound to make different pitches.
1.0	With help, partial success at level 2.0 content and level 3.0 content	
0.0	Even with help, no understanding demonstrated	

Elementary Nonexample of Using Student-Generated Scales

The elementary nonexample teacher has a similar activity in mind and is on track to an effective lesson. However, she fails to model the process as the example teacher did for students. She dismisses students to work in their groups before they have seen a model of the personalized goal they are to create. This one instructional decision took the lesson off track.

Secondary Example of Using Student-Generated Scales

The secondary example showing the use of student-generated scales in the classroom is focused on the following math standard: *Know the formulas for the area and circumference of a circle and use them to solve problems; give an informal derivation of the relationship between the circumference and area of a circle* (CCSS.Math.7.G.B.4). In preparation for using student-generated scales in her classroom, the teacher has generated a performance scale based on the standard. Figure 4.5 displays this performance scale.

Figure 4.5: Teacher-Created Performance Scale for Seventh-Grade Mathematics

Middle School – Mathematics	Grade: Seventh
(CCSS.Math.7.G.B.4): Know the formulas for the area and circumference of a circle and use them to solve problems; give an informal derivation of the relationship between the circumference and area of a circle.	

4.0	Students will be able to: ● **Solve** multistep, complex problems involving the use of formulas for area and circumference of circles

3.0	Students will be able to:
	● **Know** the formulas for the area and circumference of a circle and use them to solve problems
	   – **Calculate** the area and circumference of a circle using a formula
	   – **Solve** text-based problems involving area and circumference using formulas
	
	● **Describe** the relationship between the circumference and area of a circle
	   – **Explain** the ratio of the circumference to the diameter of a circle is always the same. The value of the ratio is *C/d* or pi (π = 22/7, 3.14, slightly greater than 3)
	   – **Explain** the relationship between circumference and area in a circle

2.0	Students will be able to **recognize** and **recall** vocabulary, including: ● *area, circumference, circle, diameter, radius, pi (π), ratio, two-dimensional* Students will be able to: ● **Recognize** and **recall** formulas for area and circumference of circles ● **Calculate** diameter and radius ● **Identify** problems in which formulas for area and circumference of circles would be needed
1.0	With help, partial success at level 2.0 content and level 3.0 content
0.0	Even with help, no understanding demonstrated

She then develops a template for students that provides structure for their scale and supports their creation of a scale. In the example that follows in Figure 4.6, the teacher furnishes a template to guide the process that includes the teacher scale on the left and an area on the right for the students to record their personalized learning targets related to the targets and content.

Figure 4.6: Template for Student-Generated Performance Scale

	Middle School – Mathematics	Grade: Seventh
	(CCSS.Math.7.G.B.4): Know the formulas for the area and circumference of a circle and use them to solve problems; give an informal derivation of the relationship between the circumference and area of a circle.	

Level	Teacher-Created Performance Scale	Student-Generated Scale Template
4.0	Students will be able to: • **Solve** multistep complex problems involving the use of formulas for area and circumference of circles	**I will** solve multistep complex problems involving the use of formulas for area and circumference of circles as it relates to my personalized learning target.

3.0	Students will be able to:
	• **Know** the formulas for the area and circumference of a circle and use them to solve problems
	  – **Calculate** the area and circumference of a circle using a formula
	  – **Solve** text-based problems involving area and circumference using formulas
	
	• **Describe** the relationship between the circumference and area of a circle
	  – **Explain** the ratio of the circumference to the diameter of a circle is always the same. The value of the ratio is C/d or pi (π = 22/7, 3.14, slightly greater than 3)
	  – **Explain** the relationship between circumference and area in a circle
		I will achieve all of the 3.0 targets on the teacher scale to achieve my personalized learning target below and:

2.0	Students will be able to **recognize** and **recall** vocabulary, including: • *area, circumference, circle, diameter, radius, pi (π), ratio, two-dimensional* Students will be able to: • **Recognize** and **recall** formulas for area and circumference of circles • **Calculate** diameter and radius • **Identify** problems in which formulas for area and circumference of circles would be needed	**I will achieve all of the 2.0 targets on the teacher scale to achieve my personalized learning target.** **Additional vocabulary or targets required:**
1.0	With help, partial success at level 2.0 content and level 3.0 content	
0.0	Even with help, no understanding demonstrated	

After each level in the learning progression and the related content are explained, questions pertaining to the unit of study are answered. A discussion about various circular objects and the application of area and circumference in the real world ensues. The teacher asks students, "What are some things related to circles that you are interested in learning more about?" The students then brainstorm possible topics of interest related to circles, circumference, area, or pi with a partner, and then share their ideas with the class. After time for reflection and research, students are asked to document their chosen personalized learning target on a scale template provided by the teacher. The teacher explains the process:

> Now that you have had time to determine a topic you are interested in learning more about related to our study of circles, I would like you to create a personal learning target. This target will be placed at level 3.0 on the right-hand side of the template I provided. Notice that your student-generated learning target will not replace the other targets on the teacher scale. Everyone is responsible for learning and understanding the teacher targets on the left. These learning targets will in fact support you as you strive to reach your related personal goal. The target you place on the right side personalizes your learning journey and creates a focus and a reason for your learning.

After this introduction, the teacher goes on to explain more details about the assignment:

> Let's talk about how to word your target. All of the targets that you create must match the level of thinking shown in the targets I created from the standard. You may find it easier to use the same verbs or actions that are used in the teacher scale. In this case, your personalized goal should be to know, calculate, solve, describe, or explain the topic that interests you. Using the sentence stem "I will," write your learning target on the template. You may wish to write your learning target in the form of a question to create a learning quest instead of a learning target goal. That would be fine with me. I

will come around and view your personal target goals to verify they are related to the content from the teacher scale and that they include the same level of thinking. As I'm circulating, think about any research that may be required or questions you may need to answer to achieve your learning target.

The teacher circulates and scans the students' individual learning targets and provides feedback where needed. Once the student-generated level 3.0 target goals have been reviewed, the teacher asks the students to study the level 2.0 targets from the teacher scale and add related targets or vocabulary necessary to achieve their personal targets. For most students, the 2.0 targets will be the same for both the teacher- and student-generated scales, with only vocabulary terms related to the personalized target being added.

After the related 2.0 targets have been generated, the teacher holds a similar discussion regarding the generation of the level 4.0 target. The teacher explains that level 4.0 on the progression of learning is meant to extend learning beyond the initial target goal and therefore is more complex. A generic statement connecting the student's personalized learning target to the teacher-created level 4.0 learning target is already provided on the template. The students are told they can either use this generic target or create a more personalized level 4.0 target that is specifically related to their generated level 3.0 target. The teacher offers to provide assistance and guidance for those students who are interested in further personalizing their level 4.0 targets. The scales are collected and reviewed by the teacher one last time to verify alignment to both the content and cognitive complexity outlined in the teacher-related scale. Figure 4.7 is an example of a completed template that includes student-generated targets.

Figure 4.7: Student-Generated Performance Scale

Middle School – Mathematics		Grade: Seventh

(CCSS.Math.7.G.B.4): Know the formulas for the area and circumference of a circle and use them to solve problems; give an informal derivation of the relationship between the circumference and area of a circle.

Level	Teacher-Created Performance Scale	Student-Generated Scale
4.0	Students will be able to: • **Solve** multistep complex problems involving the use of formulas for area and circumference of circles	**I will** solve multistep complex problems involving the use of formulas for area and circumference of circles as it relates to my personalized learning target. **I will determine** which material I can afford on my $60 budget.

3.0	Students will be able to:
	• **Know** the formulas for the area and circumference of a circle and use them to solve problems
	  – **Calculate** the area and circumference of a circle using a formula
	  – **Solve** text-based problems involving area and circumference using formulas
	• **Describe** the relationship between the circumference and area of a circle
	  – **Explain** the ratio of the circumference to the diameter of a circle is always the same. The value of the ratio is *C/d* or pi (π = 22/7, 3.14, slightly greater than 3).
	  – **Explain** the relationship between circumference and area in a circle
		I will achieve all of the 3.0 targets on the teacher scale to achieve my personalized learning target below and:
		
		• **I will calculate** the circumference of a circular flowerbed that I want to put under the tree in my front yard.
		• **I will know** how much border material I need by researching different landscaping material (border, bricks, stones, etc.) that can be used for my project.
		• **I will calculate** the area of my flowerbed to determine how much mulch I need.

2.0	Students will be able to **recognize** and **recall** vocabulary, including: • *area, circumference, circle, diameter, radius, pi (π), ratio, two-dimensional* Students will be able to: • **Recognize** and **recall** formulas for area and circumference of circles • **Calculate** diameter and radius • **Identify** problems in which formulas for area and circumference of circles would be needed	**I will achieve all of the 2.0 targets on the teacher scale to achieve my personalized learning target.** **Additional vocabulary or targets required:** landscaping terms
1.0	With help, partial success at level 2.0 content and level 3.0 content	
0.0	Even with help, no understanding demonstrated	

Secondary Nonexample of Using Student-Generated Scales

In the nonexample, the same teacher-created scale on circles is presented to the students in the class, and the concept of a student-generated scale is introduced as follows:

> I have just handed out a copy of the performance scale for our study of circles. Today, I want you to create your own scale for this unit of study. After looking over the scale I gave you, think about a topic of your choice that is related to the content we will cover during our study of circles. That topic will become your personalized learning target at level 3.0 on your scale. Simply refer to the other targets on the scale I provided and create the rest of your targets, personalizing them along the way. You may either handwrite or use the computer to type up your personalized scale. When you are finished with your scale, place it on the corner of my desk. I will return it after I review and document your personal goal choice.

The nonexample teacher does not provide a template or another supportive structure for students to follow other than the teacher-created scale itself. The students are asked to generate a personal version of the scale about a topic of their choice related to the content to be covered. There is no evidence that the teacher has explained the teacher-created targets and scale prior to the activity. It appears that the teacher does not offer or provide enough contextual support to ensure the students understand the purpose of the task or how to successfully generate a personalized scale. There is no explanation of aligning the targets to the cognitive complexity or rigor of the original teacher scale. No time was provided for discussion, research, or reflection. Lastly, the teacher did state the scales would be reviewed, but did not validate the connection to the required learning. They would be reviewed solely to document the students' personal goal choices.

Determining If Students Understand the Student-Generated Scale

Fostering self-efficacy and independent learning is an admirable ambition; however, without some type of structure (e.g., template, outline, sentence stems, or question starters), the construction of personalized learning targets that correlate with compulsory content can be problematic. Effective student-generated scales derive from a great deal of teacher support and guidance. To substantiate student success in this area, a teacher must witness behaviors that indicate viable connections to the content are being established. Teachers must closely review students' final scale product and continue to listen and watch as students interact with the content. Following is a list of ways you can monitor whether your students are making personal connections with the content that demonstrate an understanding of the learning target goal and scale.

- Ask students to share their student-generated scales with a partner and have them evaluate each other's scales to verify alignment to the teacher-created targets and scale. Circulate and listen to the conversations, interacting and asking questions as the need arises.

- After instruction of each target in the teacher-created scale, ask the students to complete a one-sentence summary explaining the connection of the presented information to the personalized targets on their scales.

- Have students make an entry in their learning log or journal sharing the impact generating a personalized learning target has had on their motivation and propensity to learn. Collect the logs or journals and review each entry.

- Group students with similar personalized targets together, and ask each group to create a poster or nonlinguistic representation of their personalized learning targets compared to the compulsory content targets from the teacher scale.

- Create a gesture that can be used to signal when a connection or link has been made between the compulsory content and a student's personal learning target. Ask students to use the gesture during instruction to signal they made a connection and have linked the content to their personal learning target.

The student proficiency scale for student-generated scales in Table 4.1 will help you determine how well your students are progressing in making personal connections with the content that demonstrate an understanding of the learning goal target and scale. Use this scale to help you monitor for this connected understanding of the learning targets and the progression of the scale.

Table 4.1: Student Proficiency Scale for Student-Generated Scales

Emerging	Fundamental	Desired Result
Students provide responses to create a personalized learning target at level 3.0.	Students provide responses to create a personalized learning target at level 3.0 that accurately connects to the content at level 3.0 of the teacher-created scale.	Students provide responses to generate a personalized learning target at all levels of the scale that accurately connects to the content and is at the same level of cognitive complexity as the teacher-created target(s) and scale.
Students can identify some of the connections between their student-generated targets and scale and the teacher-created targets and scale.	Students can list the connections between their student-generated targets and scale and the teacher-created targets and scale.	Students can explain the connections between their student-generated targets and scale and the teacher-created targets and scale.
Students can explain how the presented content relates to a specific teacher-created learning target.	Students can explain how the presented content relates to a specific student-generated learning target.	Students can explain how the presented content relates to the progression of learning of all of the targets related in the student-generated scale.
Student understanding of the learning targets, goal, and what the student-generated scale means is sometimes inaccurate and incomplete.	Student understanding of the learning targets, goal, and what the student-generated scale means is accurate but sometimes incomplete.	Student understanding of the learning targets, goal, and what the student-generated scale means is accurate and all-inclusive.

Scaffold and Extend Instruction to Meet Students' Needs

Meeting the needs of all students while creating and implementing student-generated scales in your classroom requires intentional planning from both teachers and students. Some students may find it easy to delve into generating a personal learning target and scale, while others may struggle with taking control of their learning and the self-direction the process entails. For the desired result to be met, you may need to employ adaptations to meet the individual needs of your students. The following examples can be used as a springboard when providing adaptations to help students understand and use student-generated scales.

Scaffolding

- If students struggle with determining their personal target goal, model the thought process necessary to find a personal connection with the content. Provide a list of ways students can link personal interests or ambitions to the content (e.g., athletics, future career possibilities, projects of interest, individual ambitions, hobbies, beliefs, etc.).

- Provide concrete guidance to students who need it. Conduct one-to-one conferences to probe and discover individual interests. Explain the general theme to be studied and encourage students to focus on something related to the general theme versus the individual learning targets on the scale.

- For students who struggle with the autonomous nature of learning required with student-generated scales, allow them to partner with another student with a similar personal goal and work together to make connections between the presented content and their personal learning target.

Extending

- Ask students to display the process they plan to follow to attain their personalized learning target on a poster and post it in the classroom as an example for others to view.

- Ask students to act as a mentor for students who need help setting a personalized goal. Have them develop a series of questions to guide the generation process for other students.

Conclusion

The goal of this guide is to enable teachers to become more effective in teaching students to attain critical academic standards by creating and using learning targets and performance scales in the classroom.

To determine if this goal has been met, you will need to gather information from your students, as well as solicit feedback from your supervisor or colleagues, to find someone willing to embark on this learning journey with you. Engage in a meaningful self-reflection on your use of the strategy. If you acquire nothing else from this guide, let it be the importance of *monitoring*. The tipping point in your level of expertise and your students' achievement is *monitoring*. Implementing this strategy well is not enough. Your goal is the desired result: evidence that your students have developed deeper understanding of the content.

To be most effective, view implementation as a three-step process:

1. Implement the strategy using your energy and creativity to adopt and adapt the various techniques in this guide.

2. Monitor for the desired result. In other words, while you are implementing a technique, determine whether that technique is effective with the students.

3. If, as a result of your monitoring, you realize that your instruction was not adequate for students to achieve the desired result, seek out ways to change and adapt.

Although you can certainly experience this guide and gain expertise independently, the process will be more beneficial if you read and work through the contents with colleagues.

Reflection and Discussion Questions

Use the following reflection and discussion questions during a team meeting or even as food for thought prior to a meeting with your coach, mentor, or supervisor:

1. How has your instruction changed as a result of reading and implementing the instructional techniques found in this guide?

2. What ways have you found to modify and enhance the instructional techniques found in this guide to scaffold and extend your instruction?

3. What was your biggest challenge, in terms of implementing this instructional strategy?

4. How would you describe the changes in your students' learning that have occurred as a result of implementing this instructional strategy?

5. What will you do to share what you have learned with colleagues at your grade level or in your department?

References

Common Core State Standards Initiative. (2010). *Common Core State Standards for English language arts & literacy in history/social studies, science, and technical subjects.* Retrieved March 19, 2015, from http://www.corestandards.org/assets /CCSSI_ELA%20Standards.pdf

Common Core State Standards Initiative. (2010). *Common Core State Standards for mathematics.* Retrieved March 19, 2015, from http://www.corestandards.org /wp-content/uploads/Math_Standards.pdf

CPALMS, Florida Center for Research in Science, Technology, Engineering & Mathematics, Learning Systems Institute, Florida State University. Retrieved March 19, 2015, from http://www.cpalms.org/Public/Search /CriteriaSearch?search=Standards&subjectId=29&gradeId=14

English Language Arts and Reading Texas Essential Knowledge and Skills (TEKS). *Chapter 110. Texas Essential Knowledge and Skills for English Language Arts and Reading, Subchapter B. Middle School.* Retrieved March 26, 2015, from http://ritter.tea.state.tx.us/rules/tac/chapter110/ch110b.html

Hattie, J. (2008). *Visible learning: A synthesis of over 800 meta-analyses relating to achievement.* New York: Routledge.

Hom, H. L., Jr., & Murphy, M. D. (1983). Low achiever's performance: The positive impact of a self-directed goal. *Personality and Social Psychology Bulletin, 11*, 275–285.

Marzano, R. J. (2007). *The art and science of teaching: A comprehensive framework for effective instruction.* Alexandria, VA: Association for Supervision and Curriculum Development.

Marzano, R. J. (2009). *Designing & teaching learning goals & objectives.* Bloomington, IN: Marzano Research Laboratory.

Marzano, R. J. (2013, November). Art and science of teaching: Planning for what student's don't know. *Educational Leadership, 71*(3), 80–81.

Marzano, R. J., Boogren, T., Heflebower, T., Kanold-McIntyre, J., & Pickering, D. (2012). *Becoming a reflective teacher.* Bloomington, IN: Marzano Research Laboratory.

Marzano, R. J., & Brown, J. L. (2009). *A handbook for the art and science of teaching.* Alexandria, VA: Association for Supervision and Curriculum Development.

Marzano, R. J., & Kendall, J. S. (2007). *The New Taxonomy of educational objectives* (2nd ed.). Thousand Oaks, CA: Corwin.

Marzano, R. J., & Kendall, J. S. (2008). *Designing & assessing educational objectives: Applying the New Taxonomy.* Thousand Oaks, CA: Corwin.

Marzano, R. J., & Toth, M. D. (2013). *Deliberate practice for deliberate growth: Teacher evaluation systems for continuous instructional improvement.* West Palm Beach, FL: Learning Sciences International.

Marzano, R. J., Yanoski, D. C., Hoegh, J. K., Simms, J. A., Heflebower, T., & Warrick, P. (2013). *Using Common Core State Standards to enhance classroom instruction and assessment.* Bloomington, IN: Marzano Research Laboratory.

National Council for the Social Studies (NCSS). (2013). *The College, Career, and Civic Life (C3) Framework for Social Studies State Standards: Guidance for enhancing the rigor of K–12 civics, economics, geography, and history.* Silver Spring, MD: NCSS. Retrieved March 19, 2015, from http://education.nationalgeographic.com /media/file/C3-Framework-for-Social-Studies.pdf

Rao, S. M., & Gagie, B. (2006, July/August). Learning through seeing and doing: Visual supports for children with autism. *TEACHING Exceptional Children, 38*(6) 26–33.

Stiggins, R., Arter, J., Chappuis, J., & Chappuis, S. (2006). *Classroom assessment for student learning: Doing it right—using it well.* Upper Saddle River, NJ: Pearson Education.

Tomlinson, C. A. (2014). *The differentiated classroom: Responding to the needs of all learners* (2nd ed.). Alexandria, VA: Association for Supervision and Curriculum Development.

Tomlinson, C. A. (2000, August). *Differentiation of instruction in the elementary grades.* Retrieved from ERIC database. (ED443572).

Virginia Department of Education. (2010). *Science Standards of Learning for Virginia Public Schools.* Retrieved March 19, 2015, from http://www.doe.virginia.gov /testing/sol/standards_docs/science/

Index

A

academic standard, defined, 8

analysis, 27, 28

B

basic processes, defined, 8

C

CCR (College and Career Readiness) Anchor Standards, defined, 2

CCSS (Common Core State Standards), 3

    defined, 2

chunking standards, 15–16

cognitive complexity, determining, 28–29

cognitively complex targets

    creating, 21–22

    defined, 8, 13

    examples of, 22–23

    inserting, 39–40

comprehension, 27, 28

content, defined, 2

D

declarative knowledge

    defined, 8, 10–11

    foundational targets for, 12

    identifying, 14–15

desired result

    See also name of instructional technique

    defined, 2

E

extending, defined, 2

extending instruction. *See name of instructional technique*

F

foundational targets

    defined, 8, 11–13

    examples of, 19–21, 35

    integration of, 34–36

    unpacking, 18

H

Hom, H. L., Jr., 89

I

instructional strategies, defined, 2

instructional techniques

    See also name of instructional technique

    defined, 2

K

knowledge

    See also declarative knowledge; procedural knowledge

    utilization, 27, 28

L

learning goal, defined, 8

learning goal targets

    defined, 8, 11

Notes

Notes

Notes

Notes

Notes

Notes

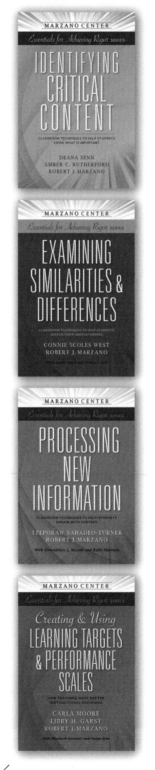
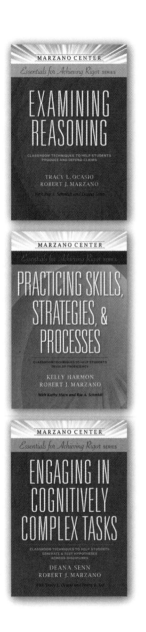